Lord Norton

**High and Low Church by Lord Norton**

Second Edition

Lord Norton

**High and Low Church by Lord Norton**
*Second Edition*

ISBN/EAN: 9783743330184

Manufactured in Europe, USA, Canada, Australia, Japa

Cover: Foto ©Lupo / pixelio.de

Manufactured and distributed by brebook publishing software (www.brebook.com)

Lord Norton

**High and Low Church by Lord Norton**

# HIGH AND LOW CHURCH

BY

LORD NORTON

*SECOND EDITION*

London
PERCIVAL & CO.
1893

# CONTENTS

|  | PAGE |
|---|---|
| Definitions, | 1 |
| History— | 3 |
|     Councils, | 5 |
|     East and West Divisions, | 6 |
|     Reformation, | 7 |
|     The English Church, | 9 |
| Two Natures of the Human Mind, | 10 |
| Two Church Parties, | 11 |
| The Terms High and Low Church, | 13 |
| High and Low Church tendencies balance each other, and alternately predominate, | 14 |
| Dissent, | 18 |
| Church Parties distinct from Dissenters | 21 |
| High and Low Views of the Church— | 22 |
|     Special High Church Views, | 22 |
|     Special Low Church Views, | 23 |
|     Comparison of the two Views, | 24 |
| High and Low Views of Church Ministry— | 25 |
|     Absolution, | 26 |
|     Confession, | 27 |
|     Preaching, | 28 |
| High and Low Views of Church Service— | 29 |
|     Of Baptism, | 29 |
|     High Church Views, | 29 |
|     Low Church Views, | 30 |
|     Comparison, | 31 |
|     The Lord's Supper, | 32 |
|     High Church Views, | 34 |
|     Low Church Views, | 36 |
|     Reflections, | 36 |
|     Fasting Communion, | 37 |

|  | PAGE |
|---|---|
| On Fasting in General, | 38 |
| Saints' Days, | 41 |
| Ritual, | 43 |
| Lincoln Judgment. | 46 |
|     Mixed Chalice, | 46 |
|     Candles, | 48 |
|     Eastward Position, | 49 |
|     Agnus Dei, | 50 |
|     General Reflections, | 50 |
| The Difference of High and Low Church Views, though *not Vital*, are *not Unimportant*, | 52 |
| Fundamental Christian Doctrine is held in Common, | 54 |
| The Difference of High and Low Church Views is Inseparable from Human Nature, | 57 |
| Via Media, | 58 |
| Christian Life is the Common Aim, | 60 |
| Prayers for Unity, | 61 |
| High and Low Church Views may have nothing to do with Religion, | 62 |
| The Mass of Christians in the World are outside any Visible Church, | 64 |
| But Voluntary Outsiders not without Guilt, | 65 |
| Church Parties' Conflict in the presence of a Common Foe, | 66 |
| The Church, as the world widens, needs stronger Bonds of Union, | 68 |
| But Catholicity forbids Identity both in Corporate and Individual Communion, | 70 |
| True Christian Fellowship, | 71 |

# HIGH AND LOW CHURCH.

### Definitions.

WANT of definition is the life of all controversy: and controversy is the bane of Christian spirit, of which unity is the essential characteristic, and large comprehensiveness the most distinguishing quality.

The following discussion relates to differences of views within the Church, as to matters connected with its doctrine and practice.

'The Church,' in its widest sense, means a community 'belonging to the Lord.' Such acceptation its Greek etymology implies.

Within this description come all the Faithful of the human race under every Divine dispensation, from that of the first promise of redemption from the 'Fall' to the covenant with Abraham, and the law given on Mount Sinai, up to the rising of the Light on Zion which brought mankind out of darkness to the full revelation of the Kingdom of the Son of God.

The spirits of the justified in disembodied state 'waiting for the adoption, to wit, the redemption of the body' (Rom. viii. 19), and the militant still in earth's probation, are in this communion with The Lord, and with each other, 'out of every kindred, tongue, people, and nation' (Rev. v. 9).

'The Christian Church' means the visible institution of Christ on earth, as organised by His Apostles. This is the recognised depositary of Christian doctrine, and the divinely appointed channel of Christian grace.

As a visible association, it has its terms of admission

by baptism—'we are all baptized into one body,'—its badges of membership, and its accredited Ministry and Services. Repentance, faith, and obedience are its vital conditions, amidst much affectation of a vain profession. Many professed members of the body are not of its true spirit, but only formally admitted and nominally enlisted in it. Many good Christians, on the other hand, are of its spirit who have not been formally incorporated. Some are even in avowed separation from it, and in independent communities. Such may, nevertheless, be virtually in fellowship with the mystical body of which Christ is the Head—'the blessed company of all faithful people.' The Church charitably assumes all communicants to be its members. No more than this is cognisable to human ken. The Searcher of hearts alone discriminates the true members from the false; and even He leaves the actual severance to final issue.

Dr. Pusey thus beautifully draws this distinction: 'They are members of the Soul of the Church who, though not of the visible Body, unknowingly reject the ordinances of Christ; but in faith, love, and obedience cleave to Him. And many members of the Body are not members of the Soul of the Church, who, amid outward profession of the faith, do in heart and deed deny Him whom in words they worship. The promise of deliverance is for those who, in the Body of the Church, belong also in faith and love to the Soul, and to those who, though, not by their own fault, out of the Body, belong to the Soul, cleaving to the Lord.' (*Minor Prophets*, Joel ii. 32: '*Whosoever shall call on the name of the Lord shall be delivered*').

The 19th Article defines the visible Church of Christ as a congregation of faithful men, in which the pure Word of God is preached, and the holy Sacraments are duly administered.

The Christian Church is catholic—that is, open to all and intended to embrace all, mankind. It is *potentially* the right and privilege of everybody to belong to it, and none are inadmissible or aliens to it involuntarily. Christ invites all to come to Him—Himself the way. All may take shelter in the ' Ark of His Covenant ' from the approaching deluge of this world's ungodliness. It is offered as the refuge for all from a common danger, and the conductor to a common destiny of redemption from it.

The English Church is a Branch of this Catholic Church. It is the aggregate of all our countrymen who have been baptized into it.

## History.

The Jewish Church was of a single nation, selected for a rallying standard from the world's confusion. It was the depositary of the sacred promises of redemption to mankind, from God's blessing to Abraham, to the 'lively oracles' in the wilderness, through the voices of the Prophets up to John the Baptist, who heralded the 'Lord Himself coming suddenly to His temple, even the Messenger of the Covenant' (Malachi iii. 1). At the crisis of redemption the veil of the temple was rent in twain, and all men saw the mystery which from the beginning 'had been hid in God' according to the eternal purpose which He purposed in Christ Jesus our Lord, of whom the whole family in heaven and earth is named. (Eph. iii. 9).

When He died it was not for that nation only, but He gathered together in one the children of God that were scattered abroad (John xi. 52).

He had sent forth His twelve Apostles to preach His Gospel first to the house of Israel; and, after He left this earth, His Spirit descended visibly on them, and every man heard it in his own language.

So sprang the Christian Church from Christ Himself, which His Apostles organised with constituted Ministry, Ordinances, and the divinely ordained Sacraments; and thousands rapidly came into their fellowship.

At first it formed itself in separate societies located in every place of the Apostles' operations. Each such society was called a church, even if consisting of one household only; and the aggregate was called the Church of Christ. So it was said that 'prayers were made for Peter *by the Church*;' and in another place the Apostles were 'brought on their way *by the Church*;' and the word 'church' occurs in both senses where it is said that 'it pleased the Apostles and Elders, with the whole Church, to send chosen men to the church at Antioch.'

Epistles were written to the church at Corinth, and to the church of Galatia, and to the church of the Thessalonians; and the Revelation of Christ by St. John to the seven churches of Asia. As the Apostles went through the cities they delivered them the decrees for to keep that were ordained in Jerusalem, and so were the churches established in the faith, and increased in number daily (Acts xvi. 5).

They became gradually collected into dioceses under Bishops, and afterwards were grouped in provincial areas under Patriarchs. James was the first Bishop of Jerusalem, Timothy of Ephesus, Titus of Crete.

There was no supremacy among the Apostles nor among the churches. Christendom never was an earthly monarchy, Christ alone being the Universal Head. The Apostolic Council at Jerusalem, over which St. James presided, became naturally the seat of advice and reference. Jewish Christians were, in fact, for a time, under a double system. St. Paul had care of all the churches, and was specially the Apostle of the Gentiles, as St. Peter was of the Jews. St. Paul once rebuked St. Peter for compelling Gentiles to live as Jews; but in his contention with Barnabas, who was not one of the twelve, he had no power to decide, but separated himself.

In spite of bitter hostility from without, and false brethren within, the Church wonderfully preserved, even in its first scattered state, without any *coercive* authority, unanimity in the Apostolic doctrine and fellowship. Nothing short of Divine superintendence can account for this. The churches thus became independent witnesses to the truth. The sustained identity of their Articles of Faith, and their uniformity of practice, gave most striking proof to all the world of common origin, and of communion with one Spirit and one Lord who had promised to be with them always—though unseen—to the end.

This is the real unity of the Christian Church visible on earth.

The ramifications from the sacred stem, breaking out in solitary shoots at first, soon spreading in large branches throughout the world, constitute the Church's catholicity. The supposition of a leadership in any branch is a denial of the central stem, and a confusion of view which has misled even great minds to wander in the search for a vain ideal of unity.

The destruction of Jerusalem so soon after our Lord's Ascension prevented any habit of reference for counsel from growing into a feeling of dependence on central authority (Bishop Fitzgerald's *Lectures*). Catholicity is an antithesis to centralisation in the idea of the Christian Church.

The break-up of Jewish Polity synchronised with Gentile intercommunication, and the promulgation of universal Christianity. The everlasting Kingdom was then set up which was prophesied by Daniel (vii. 14), and the entrance to which, through repentance and faith, was preached by the Forerunner's voice, and then by Christ Himself. Then began what will ultimately become the Church triumphant in heaven: a great multitude which no man can number, of all nations (Rev. vii. 9.)

## *Councils.*

The conferences of the Apostles and Elders under the guidance of the Holy Ghost (Acts xv. 28) were followed by ' Œcumenical Councils' and Provincial Episcopal Synods.

The first Œcumenical Council was held at Nice, A.D. 325, to adjudicate on the Arian heresy concerning our Lord's Divinity.

There were only six such Councils of the whole Church.

## East and West Divisions.

When the centre of empire removed to Constantinople the Church got divided East and West.

The Bishop of Rome then asserted a supremacy over the Western Church; and the Council of Chalcedon confirmed the jurisdiction of the See of Constantinople.

There was however in this division no *Schism* of the Body. The Greek and Latin Churches were two groups, both in the communion of the Catholic Church (W. Palmer, *Church*, i. 153). The Council held at Constantinople, A.D. 864, was recognised by both East and West as œcumenical.

The Eastern Church inclined most to speculative theology, and was specially called 'Orthodox;' while the Western assumed the title of 'Catholic,' and evinced the Roman turn for government and empire. *Hæ tibi erunt artes.*

The Greek and Roman faculties have always contrasted each other in their respective absence and possession of administrative power; and so, in the two Churches, the spirit of doctrinal controversy and that of ceremonial discipline have respectively prevailed. Talleyrand quotes Napoleon to have said, in conversation on the principal efforts of the human mind, ' Le développement rapide du Christianisme avait opéré une réaction admirable de l'esprit grec contre l'esprit romain. La Grèce vaincue par la force physique s'occupait de la conquête de l'empire intellectuel qu'elle avait effectivé en saisissant le germe bienfaiteur qui a eu tant d'influence sur l'humanité entière ' (*Mémoire*, i. 435).

The Eastern Church became the asylum of theological learning while barbarians were ravaging the West; and afterwards the Latin Church became the great scene of political and ecclesiastical power throughout the world.

Constantine's establishment of Christianity, and the removal of empire, gave the Bishop of Rome Western preeminence, civil and ecclesiastical; and the Augustine theology, derived from Africa, characterised the Romish Church with what is called Sacerdotalism.

The Councils of the fourth century, however, show (to quote words of Mr. Gladstone in his review of *Ecce Homo*) that 'after many a fearful reel, a nearly unanimous Christendom settled down upon a centre of gravity in doctrinal expression which has been stable through the vicissitudes of 1500 years; and which to all appearance nothing can now shake, unless there comes a shock under which all definite Christianity should crumble. The combined belief in the divinity and humanity of Christ has survived the strain of all the convulsive forces which rent East from West, and which then broke off from the great Western map so many integral parts of its articulated structure, and which have disorganised so much of what they did not actually sever.'

## Reformation.

The union of temporal and spiritual power in the Pope led to mischief in the Western Church. St. Bernard, its most zealous defender, deplored the growing corruptions, A.D. 1100, and asked, 'Is it devotion that now wears out the Apostolical threshold, or is it ambition? The unsavoury contagion spreads throughout the Church. The ministers of Christ are the servants of Antichrist.' What he stigmatised as meretricious splendour, and the abuses of exemptions and indulgences, and all the corruptions of superstition and idolatry, culminated in the convulsions of the fifteenth century, and precipitated the Reformation.

Bishop Creighton observes of this great and wide reaction, that 'it was not one definite event, but a slowly gathered result. The Papal autocracy gave way to new conceptions, political, intellectual, and religious' (*History of the Papacy*). Politically viewed, it was an assertion of State independence against Church claims of supremacy. It was a joint protest against usurpation and corruption.

England was the first country to show a spirit of national resistance to foreign interference, combined with the protest against ecclesiastical and religious corruption. When Henry VIII. was invited to head the League for the Confession of Augsburg he was bent on his private quarrel with Leo, which so fortunately gave this nation their opportunity to acquire the emancipation they had long been struggling for. No sooner, indeed, had the King achieved his own private object, than he made clear his distinction between its religious and political aspects. As 'Defender of the Faith' he promulgated the 'Six Articles,' which vindicated, under frightful penalties, the worst corruptions of Rome, while he was renouncing its jurisdiction.

Europe became divided between adherents and abhorrents of Papal supremacy. The former were chiefly nationalities of the warmer Celtic and Italian blood; the latter, of the colder German and Teutonic race: the two being distinguished by their dispositions, in matter of religion, either by an excess of superstition, or of rationalism.

Elaborate ecclesiasticism, and a frigid simplicity, were the respective characteristics of the two religious systems. 'It became,' says Dr. Vaughan (*Revolution*, iii. 3), 'the resolve of the Teutonic races, and especially of Englishmen, that their religion should no longer be something external and artificial, but something inward and real.'

The admixture of Celtic, Saxon, and Norman blood in English veins gave both sternness and fervour to the religious revolution in this country. This mixture of race gave a peculiar turn to the struggle of the sixteenth century in England.

## The English Church.

So issued the independent English branch of the Catholic Church, with its own canons, jurisdiction, and rights; and recognising the king as its supreme earthly head.

'The privileges of the Clergy,' says Blackstone, 'were necessarily abridged by the Reformation, owing to the ill use made of them by the Popish priests.' The laws of England were the last appeal in all ecclesiastical causes. The Church in England is no *imperium in imperio*; and its self-legislation, like the bye-laws of any corporation, must submit to the surveillance of the supreme tribunal, to keep it within its authorised limits, and to its letter.

Dr. Pusey describes the English Church, which was originally Greek, as 'having assumed, after the Roman mission of Augustine, a Latin character, and so embracing in its authoritative recognition the Fathers of both Eastern and Western Churches.' It is the folly of many to talk of circumstantial phases of the Christian Church as of different religions. The Reformation introduced no new faith, though the blindness of controversy ignored the common ground of Christianity, which remained unaffected by it.

The old British Church, of still older Irish lineage, when retrieved by Romish Mission from temporary wreck under Saxon heathendom, fell under the ill effects of Romish domination, and recovered at the Reformation its pristine purity.

Pope Gregory in his celebrated colloquy with Augustine recognised its proper claim to independence, which for centuries it failed to realise.

In the revision of its Liturgy at the Reformation, nothing appears more clearly than the careful separation of Romish adjuncts from the original purely scriptural doctrine, and the desire to make no needless alteration. The difference between the English Prayer-Book and Romish Missal is the absence of special dogma imposed on original simplicity.

## Two natures of the human mind.

There are two different kinds of mental constitution, which see all things differently; one in an objective, the other in a subjective, point of view.

The different tendencies are as remarkable individually as corporately. Arnold observed 'an element in human nature, which in religion, in philosophy, and in literature, assumes in each a different form.' He thought it 'an error to suppose that either of the two tendencies so affecting the course of human affairs was simply good or bad. Each had its good and evil intermingled. Trace them from their highest springs; on one side are ideas of truth and justice; on the other, of beauty and love' (*Christian Life*, Introd. iv, 3rd ed.). They are the formalistic and æsthetic characteristics of mankind.

Macaulay says of the two great parties which have governed this country: 'The distinction has its origin in diversities of temper, of understanding, and of interest which are found in all societies, and will be found till the human mind ceases to be drawn in opposite directions by the charm of habit or of novelty; by zeal for authority and antiquity, or for liberty and progress' (*Hist.*, vol. i. p. 98, 2nd edit.).

The one class of minds naturally looks to external order and prescription for a test of right and wrong; the other looks inwardly for the impression felt. The one is submissive to authority, the other appeals to private judgment.

In politics the one class are Tory, the other Whig; in philosophy the one loves formularies, the other theory, preferring, respectively, the analytic and inductive process; in literature they are classical or utilitarian; in religion ceremonial or emotional.

At the bottom of all government, says Hallam, are two principles, stability and experiment. These two tendencies are, in the whole field of thought and action, ancillary and not antagonistic to each other. The world could not go on without both, as the planets are only kept in their orbits by the co-operation of centripetal and centrifugal forces. They may mingle in the same man, and men of each disposition often unite together in heart, and interchange their views. The same mind becomes variously affected by these two tendencies in different moods or circumstances.

## Two Church Parties.

When the Western Church was aspiring to universal rule, with demonstration of power and authority, and the Eastern turned more to theological speculation, the world ecclesiastic became accordingly divided by these two leading tendencies. At the Western Reformation the Papal grasp retained to itself those most amenable to established authority, and lost its hold on those who claimed liberty of thought.

The emancipated English Church found its members alike divided, as either of greater devotion to the concrete institution, or of more abstract yearning after the free spirit animating it. The long and bitter struggle of the Reformation exaggerated the idea of hostility between the two.

The clingers to the old Papal system as of established authority, and the more eager for its reform and purification, arranged themselves in opposite camps, and fought with such blinding fury as to lose sight of the large common ground remaining in participation between them.

Nothing shows more strikingly the intensity of this struggle than the retention to this day of the title of 'Protestant' by the freer side—as if a protest against abuse could be the permanent characteristic of any institution. It may be said that the exclusive appropriation of the title of

'Catholic' is an equal misnomer on the other side, exclusion being inconsistent with pretensions of universality.

The adherents of Rome and the champions of Reformation acquired in this country more significantly distinctive appellations as Romanist and Puritan.

Politically, the two parties were Royalist and Republican. In matter of Church government, they were Episcopalian and Independent. The battle-cry of the one was 'King and Prelacy;' and of the other 'Parliament,' and 'No Popery.' In Milton's immortal prose works there is the most eloquent retort of 'Eikonoklastes' to 'Eikon Basilike,' and the fullest expression of hatred to Prelacy. Authority and Liberty were the essentially conflicting principles throughout.

On Queen Mary's temporary re-establishment of Popery in England, and enforcement of penal laws against Reformers, many fled to Switzerland to nourish there the opposite intolerance.

Elizabeth, restoring the Reformed Church, found, according to Neal's description (*Hist. of Puritans*, Pref. iv), 'a fresh division within—some for keeping to the liturgy of King Edward, others for the fullest liberty to shake off all remains of 'Antichrist.'

Alexander Knox, whom Macaulay describes as 'a remarkable man, of great influence, of the school of Calvin, united with the theology of Arminius,' distinguishes the Lutheran and Calvinistic branches of the Reformed Church as representing respectively the Greek and Latin minds; the one bearing away from the dogmatism of Augustine to the liberality of Chrysostom, the other more exclusively narrowing to a system of their own.

The language of our Articles seems aimed to unite the theology of Luther and Melanchthon with the piety of the Primitive Church retained in our Liturgy.

In political, ecclesiastical, and doctrinal aspects, Church parties always tend to divide in the two directions—to prescription or eclecticism. The third Church party, often cited, is only an intervention between these two—a broad neutrality of any special predilection.

## The terms High and Low Church.

The Nonjurors at the Revolution were the first designated as High Church. Rather than renounce their oath of allegiance they refused to resume the benefices from which they had been ousted. They belong distinctly to the first of the two parties just described, representing, in relation to the Church, the conscientious adherence to authority against any counter claim of expediency,—the principle of allegiance against that of option of service.

Hallam describes 'the distinction of High and Low churchmen about the end of William III.'s reign, as the first being distinguished by great pretensions to sacerdotal power, both spiritual and temporal, by a repugnance to toleration and by a firm adherence to the Tory principle in the State—the latter by the opposite characteristics; and the two pitched against each other in the two houses of convocation' (*Constitutional History*, iii. 323, 3rd ed.).

The Low Church are described by Macaulay, with less impartiality, in contrast with the Nonjurors, as 'men who thought that to entitle a government to allegiance something more was necessary than mere legitimacy, or even actual possession. In their view,' he says, 'the end of all government was the happiness of society.' The Nonjurors he accuses of 'sacrificing liberty to order, and order to a superstition as stupid and degrading as the Egyptian worship of cats and onions.' He only allows that the Low Church party was fairly called latitudinarian, just as some of the Jacobites were distinguished as non-compounders (Macaulay, iii. 469).

Lord Grimthorpe has lately described the High Church party as those 'who from the first have tried to overthrow the Reformation and to restore Papacy in England.' He sympathises with the desire expressed by Disraeli for 'some middle term—some standpoint between implicit faith and freethought—an escape for civilisation from the opposing dangers of sacerdotalism and atheism.' Such was the alternative in his view.

The terms High and Low Church have been found sufficiently appropriate, to distinguish the two prevalent characteristics of men's minds in application to these great interests, to be retained ever since, through ever-changing circumstances. Certainly, neither time nor subject can confuse the two ideas of fealty with volunteer, or of obedience with inclination and self-will.

## High and Low Church Tendencies balance each other, and alternately predominate.

That would not be a national church in a free country which did not comprise men of both diversities of mental disposition.

The two propensities balance one another; and the vicissitudes of circumstance lead to their alternately predominating, and, in vigorous action, reaching the opposite extremes from the common centre.

As a pendulum in free motion swings throughout its range of oscillation from the basis of gravitation, where only restraint or stagnation causes rest, so does the mind of a free people follow recurrent impulses to and from an established basis, redressing action in opposite directions under the central attraction of their coincident loyalty.

In English Church history this alternation is remarkable. The popular spirit resists, and then recovers itself, then sways another way, and lulls again—

'*Maria alta tumescunt,*
*Rursusque in se ipsa residunt.*'

The first struggle for emancipation from the Papal incubus was checked for a time, the Court and Parliament uniting, by the Acts of Supremacy and Uniformity, to maintain ecclesiastical authority. To ridicule reformers and to preach the divine right of kings became the surest way to Church preferment.

But both Church and People soon remonstrated, the one crying Erastianism, the other Tyranny. None were pleased, and the persecuting spirit of State-Catholicism bred not only recalcitrant Protestantism but disloyalty also to the Crown.

The Reformation spirit prevailed, though the Protestants were divided between moderate reformers attached to the Church, and wholesale denouncers of clerical abuses —all, however, utterly disclaiming any imputation of schism.

The Puritans, getting ascendency, tried to impose the Covenant on the Anglican Ministry, and a Presbyterian Parliament insisted on conformity with their more exaggerated views, and slew the King. They had then their full swing till the very agency of independence itself became a tyranny, and by another reaction the Church and King recovered liberty.

The Restoration set up again the principles of loyalty, with the agreement of Convocation and acceptance of Parliament. The first Restoration-Parliament imposed on all its members, as a test, the reception of the Sacrament, and burnt the 'Solemn League and Covenant.' Charles was forced to repeal the Declaration of Indulgence, and the Test Act was passed.

In vain the Savoy Conference attempted compromise between Anglicans and Presbyterians, though their dispute regarded no vital doctrine, but only principles of government.

James II. conceived the possible restoration of Popery, but the prevailing national antipathy overpoweringly asserted itself against him.

William attempted schemes for religious comprehension. The Revolution is described by Hallam (iii. 231) as the euthanasia of religious liberty. The Act of Toleration indeed passed, but strife continued till the lethargy caused by interminable contention endangered the very life of Christianity.

Exhaustion followed on spasmodic controversy, and the eighteenth century is considered the period of the Church's lowest condition in this country—a deadly lull of strife. In that dark time of slumber came forth the spectres of infidelity, and false lights flickered over the stagnant elements.

Towards the close of the century came the 'Evangelical' revival, but its unregulated zeal broke into dissension and separations. It was however a great religious movement—a reflux of the tide of life from the lowest ebb, and a warm and genial flow. Such gatherings of Church communion as included men like Wilberforce, Gisborne, Thornton, and kindred spirits, were a great refreshment of higher feeling in this country. It was a Low Church swing of the pendulum. Their *métier* was not for restoration of forms and ceremonial. They were not the men for reconstruction of machinery, but rather for relighting the fire which had gone out, and which might again restore the motive power. It was a power, indeed, rather too strong for the then conditions of the Church machinery, and endangered its disruption. But the 'Evangelical' stirring was far from being merely spiritual. To quote Dean Church's words : 'It was especially fruitful in public results. It led Howard and Elizabeth Fry to reform our prisons, and Wilberforce to overthrow the slave-trade' (*Oxford Movement*, p. 13). The Party had sprung up within the Church at a time when free thought was strongly asserting itself in politics and literature, as well as in relation to religion. The spirit, however, was liable to evaporate, from its want of connection with systematic organisation and constitutional regulation.

Hence the next impulse was to redress the laxity of forces of self-acting Church revival. The Oxford rally, in the second quarter of the century, was a return to the High Church standard and pattern. The Prayer-Book was the standard, and the Apostolic and Patristic tradition the pattern with which all partial action was moved to conform.

In the twilight of this new dawn of reviving Church daylight Arnold and Whately were the first to stir. They recalled the Church's claim to be 'the organised body of Our Lord's institution, endowed with definite spiritual powers, but no other, whether connected with the State or not, having independent existence, and inalienable claims, and its own objects, with its own special standard, spirit, and character' (*Letters of an Episcopalian*).

But the fully awakened High Churchmen took still higher ground of claims for the Church, and quoted Our Lord's own words, 'If any man hear not the Church, let him be as a heathen:' though the Church was not instituted when that was said, nor since its institution has it ever excommunicated anybody except through the Courts after trial.

Dean Church describes the effect of such a loud appeal to Church authority as bewildering to men still in a state of half sleep; so that they indistinctly recognised, in the hasty rally, what was essentially defensible, and what not. He thought Arnold, who was the first to come forward, took no higher stand than asserting that the Church was a brotherhood of Christians, and its organisation only necessary and expedient, but not of divine authority; and that its ministry was stated, but not the mode of exercising it either as to persons, forms, or methods. His own idea of the Church was that of the full High Church revivalists, 'something very different from a State institution, claiming an origin not short of the Apostles, and speaking with their authority, and that of their Master' (*Oxford*

*Movement*, p. 7). Such High Church claims re-acted towards Popery, as the Low Church Evangelical movement had wandered towards Methodism. Both extremes avoided secession from the Church, and their differences were rather successive phases of religious life without opposition in any vital doctrine.

The Oxford impulse was an extreme High Church rebound from the Evangelical swing, and Dean Church (p. 337) thinks it led naturally to another turn which is following now, which may be called 'Church-Liberalism.'

This he calls a new party of movement, bolder and more independent, 'less inclined to put up with the traditional, more searching in its methods, more daring in its criticisms, larger in its sympathies, imaginative, enthusiastic, and, though without much of the devotional temper, penetrated by a sense of the reality of religion.' These are now the democrats of Church progress, and their principle is distinctly one of freedom. The speculative treatment of High Church tenets in *Lux Mundi* is characteristic of this latest movement.

## Dissent.

Totally distinct from all these phases of what Prebendary Curteis calls 'Church Dissension,' is the subject of Dissent.

Avowed violation of the unity of the Church by sects separating themselves in hostile and jealous rivalry, has obviously no part in this discussion.

Such disruptions of the 'One Body into which we are all baptized' began when the Reformation seemed, to shallow thinkers, a breaking up of Church authority and a scramble for a new faith by every man as seemed to him best.

As already stated, it was a time of shaken fealty, and of desire for innovation. Great discoveries were being made. The art of printing offered new facilities for intellectual communication. The schoolmaster was abroad. The northern states of Europe were developing freer government, serfdom was disappearing. Self-assertion, speculation, and diffusion of knowledge strained the hold of old allegiance whether in Church or State.

'For a hundred and fifty years before Luther an inquisitive and sectarian spirit,' says Hallam, 'began to prevail.' The Reformation, all the stronger for coming gradually, separated half Europe from the Roman See. The higher classes throughout England, and all classes in the northern and western countries, clung still to Rome; but the Reformers gained ground, and popular feeling soon rose with violence against Church assumption.

Heresies in earlier days were adjudged by Councils. The Gnostics who were lingering Judaizers, the Donatists rebels against established discipline, the Pelagians and Nestorians perverters of the doctrine of the Incarnation, and other subtler disputants, were successively condemned. After the Reformation England had her own Church documents to appeal to, to which all Churchmen were in conscience, if not by actual subscription, bound. Repudiation of the terms of the Church was rebellion against law. But in vain Elizabeth tried to enforce uniformity in practice.

The first body of Protestant Dissenters formally separating themselves from the English Church were the Independents, called also Congregationalists. They asserted as their distinctive principle a Scriptural right to complete self-government in matters of religion; throwing over all claim to organic unity in the Church. From this first secession the Baptists further seceded, illustrating the proverb that 'party breeds party,' and exhibiting the inevitable process of disintegration following from first abandonment of corporate constitution. Nonconformists fell in love with nonconformity in itself, though pronounced by Christ Himself to be a primary symptom of the absence of His Spirit, and it is a direct negative of His prayer that His Disciples might be one, as He and His Father are one. The self-asserting spirit of this world develops disunion. When Stuart Mill expressed a fear that uniformity might accompany the growth of social equality, Macaulay likened it to a cry of fire in the Deluge (*Life*, p. 257).

The Baptists were the next to secede from the Church in the seventeenth century. Doctrine became more involved in these later secessions. This, for instance, turned on Sacramental questions, and the Church's views of means of grace. London was full of Dutch Anabaptists whose recent political independence led to a kindred assertion of religious freedom. Baptists have a ritual of their own, and actually deny the validity of our Church baptism as much as Romish dissenters in England do. Spurgeon restricted their terms of admission to men at years of discretion only, and asserted that infants are not fit to be members, though Christ said all must be converted as little children. In Mr. Curteis's words, 'the Western Church was never free from the persistent error of spiritualising, and individualising away all the force and unity of Christ's Kingdom' (*Dissent*, p. 221).

The Quakers followed in order of secession, from an aversion to all ritual and outward expression of every kind, and with an assumption of exclusive spirituality.

Unitarianism, the Socinian form of Arianism, formed a schism in the Church in England in the eighteenth century. Döllinger describes it as a mechanical Calvinistic conception of the Atonement, and opposing of the Divine Persons (*Church and Churches*, p. 239). The sect is more numerous in America than here, but most of the old English Presbyterian congregations have fallen into it. Each congregation claims uncontrolled arbitrament of its own doctrine and worship, whence its very numerous subsections more or less recognising the Divinity of Our Lord.

Methodism towards the end of last century might

have been nothing more than a new religious order within the Church. But unfortunately those now calling themselves Wesleyans travesty their Founder's noble aim of Church revival to what of all things he most dreaded—Church disunion. His latest deed, still extant, limits his Ministers' appointments to three years only unless ordained in the Church; so that most of their present appointments are legally invalid. They read the same liturgy (in many places), in separation without excuse.

In Cornwall, Whitfield's chief scene of operation, they are scarcely separate from the Church; but in Wales ministerial jealousy, demagogue agitation, and chapel shareholding have so inflamed a rival spirit against the Church that they lately opposed legislation for improved clergy discipline rather than let the interests of morality strengthen the Church.

All sects have further dissected themselves in endless fragmentation. There are Methodists of many varieties, some only hiding the name of Christians under a name into which they were not baptized. The main sects call themselves 'churches,' as the several branches of the Church are properly called. The Church they consider a sect of itself, and they consider toleration, which they certainly do not mutually exercise, to mean indiscriminate impartiality without any preference of right or wrong. Such cool assumption of credit for indifference reminds one of Sheridan's sarcasm on George IV.'s boast that '*He had no predilections*'—

> '*His heart is a sieve on which dance his affections,*
> *And the finer they are the more sure to go through.*'

## Church Parties distinct from Dissenters.

The different views of High and Low Churchmen involve no schism, nor any difference on vital doctrines of Christianity, such as the Divinity of Our Lord. The divisions caused within the Church by different apprehension of the same fundamental truths by differently constituted minds come short of schism, though there is often very unchristian exaggeration of such differences causing hostile feeling, jealousies, or even mutual contempt.

That there is no vital difference of doctrine between High and Low Churchmen will best be seen by comparing their views about the Church itself, its Ministry, and its Services.

### High and Low Views of the Church.

Both parties must, in common loyalty, agree to the definition of the Visible Church in the Nineteenth Article, as 'a congregation of faithful men in the which the pure Word of God is preached, and the Sacraments are duly administered.'

And they must accept St. Paul's definition when he contrasted the true Church with the Ephesian Temple of Diana, as 'The household of God, built on the foundation of the Apostles and Prophets, Jesus Christ Himself being the chief corner-stone.'

*Special High Church Views.*

The tendency of an objective apprehension is to magnify the instrument of any achievement; as, on the other hand, the tendency of subjective appreciation is to immediate interest in the achievement itself.

There is also a common human proclivity to deify objects of sense in relief of the mental effort of faith.

The typical brazen serpent drew to itself the worship due to the Divine antitype. So, to some minds, the Church itself becomes an object of homage—almost of idolatry. Its forms and ordinances seem, to such minds, not only *means* but *ends* of devotion; and virtue is expected to proceed from mere performances. The Church, as 'the Bride of Christ,' almost takes precedence of the unseen Divinity, as a more tangible and intelligible figure for contemplation, and embodiment of worship. Such worshippers answer to the prophet's simile of fishermen sacrificing to their nets (Habakkuk i. 16). Any connection of the Church with mundane institutions seems to them a profane crastianism. The temporal headship of the sovereign, and the submission of Church legislation to civil judgment, even simply to the testing of its fidelity to its own limits, seems a giving to Cæsar of what belongs to God.

All public religious service is, in a High Church view, properly allocated to the sanctuary. For instance, the daily offering of prayer in households has no such claim to its observance as a call to any church though empty and a mile away.

The writings of the early Church Fathers, especially of Augustine's period, assume parallel authority with Scripture, while the Fathers of the Reformation fail to command the same respect as less personating the Church. These English Fathers are even accused of having tampered with the Articles to compromise the genuine church with pseudo-reformation. Moderate High Churchmen, as Dr. Hook, indeed, properly repudiate all claims of Patristic authority beyond that of contemporary evidence, such as the Apostolic Fathers certainly have of primitive times; but this falls short of High Church opinion.

The revelation of God, says Palmer (*Church*, vol. i. p. 10), only offers salvation in the name of Jesus Christ in His Church, and all men to whom the Gospel is preached must be members of this Church when sufficiently proposed to them, on pain of being excluded from the favour of God for ever.

## *Special Low Church Views.*

Bishop Ryle, whose views may be taken as typical of the best Low Church feeling, asserts that no visible church on earth can call itself the one true channel of salvation, nor assume to itself alone the true form of worship, the true church government, or the true way of administering the Sacraments. But for himself he says, 'In sincere loyal attachment to the Church of England I yield to none. I value its forms of government, its confession of faith, and its mode of worship as much as any' (*Knots Untied*, p. 268). This scarcely realises the Scriptural idea of 'the one foundation.' He says, what all, in some sense, agree in, 'that no church is sound in which the Bible is not the standard of faith and practice.' He only pronounces on his own judgment, that 'the Church is useful as a witness, keeper, and librarian of Holy Scripture' (p. 270). When he concludes that 'that is the best visible church which adds most members to the invisible,' he is confusing two ideas of a church. It is a mere truism to say that that is the best humanly visible form in which God sees most vitality, and the best outward profession which has most inward reality. This is exactly the characteristically subjective view, ignoring the means in sole contemplation of the end. Luther exclaimed against such half-conception, 'Sublime nonsense! to disregard means, in regard to the end. The devil roars out, "Spirit! spirit!" while seeking to destroy all the roads, bridges, scaling ladders, and paths by which the Spirit enters.' So Liddon, the fairest of modern theologians, said, 'Some men interest themselves in religion as an abstract good. They declaim against churches, priesthoods, fathers, creeds. The sublime essence of religion fixes their enthusiasm as a matter of feeling only. The safeguards of its practical power they consider productive of church pedantry, the external forms of a needless apparatus of scaffolding to the building.'

## Comparison of the Two Views.

Dean Church truly observes that 'the same necessities present themselves differently to different minds, and to the same mind with different impressions.' High and Low Church views cannot differ more widely than Newman's views before and after he left the English Church for Rome. He said he was attached to the one for its apostolicity, but went away to the other from an idea of its more catholicity. His bosom friend Pusey was content with the former. But Newman did not change his faith, nor Pusey his common Christian fellowship with him.

Compare, however, the cited words of Palmer and of Ryle, and widely different as the two ideas of the Church are, no article of the Creed is inconsistent with either.

Bishop Pearson, commenting on the Ninth Article— 'The Holy Catholic Church, and Communion of Saints'— makes its two divisions seem to represent in their collocation the union of the objective and subjective views of the Church, as the rock-foundation and outward bulwark of profession and discipline, and the inward communion of true devotion which God sees now within it, and which will be manifest to all in final judgment, when present shadows clear away.

## High and Low Views of Church Ministry.

One great distinction of the High Church is their view of Apostolical Succession as a continued transmission of apostolical authority and powers; the Low Church barely recognising what Dr. Hook calls a corporate lineage of Christian clergy by the consecration of bishops succeeding each other from the first Apostolic ordination.

The Preface to the Ordination Service states it to be evident to all readers of holy Scripture that from the Apostles' time there have been three orders of ministers; bishops, priests, and deacons.

The High Church clergy magnify their office beyond a ministry to somewhat of a mediatorial function, adopting in that sense St. Paul's expression, 'As ambassadors for Christ, we pray in Christ's stead.' They consider that ordination conferred on them a gift of superhuman efficacy with God on man's behalf.

*Absolution.*

As an illustration of their views, they claim the power of discerning hearts, so that on their own judgment of the penitent they can pronounce or withhold absolution. Our liturgy seems, indeed, to justify this assumption in literal adherence to the Missal. In the Ordination Service a new-made priest is told that 'Whose sins he remits they are remitted, and whose sins he retains they are retained.' And in the Visitation Service the priest, if satisfied with confession made to him, is authorised to say, 'I absolve thee.' These words, however, are shown by Bingham to have been introduced into the Service-Book in the thirteenth century, as a release from sentences of Church excommunication after penance performed; that is to say, as a remission by the Church of what the Church had imposed. He considers the words are retained in our Prayer-Book in only a deprecatory sense of God's judgment, and not as indicative of a self-asserted power of judgment and absolution.

Mr. Palmer says, 'The sacerdotal benediction of penitents was in the earlier times conveyed in the form of prayer to God for His absolution' (*Origines Liturgicæ*). In our Prayer-Book the context implies this limited intention. Dr. Hook says, 'We do not suppose that priests can discern the heart, but may only pronounce the words authoritatively in the name of God, who has committed to us the ministry of reconciliation' (*Church Dictionary, in loco*). 'The Father hath committed all judgment to the Son, because He is Son of Man.' So said Our Lord. It was, however, lately argued by an eminent preacher in a London pulpit, that when Our Lord was proving His power to forgive sins by connecting with it what the people would think the greater miracle of healing, He purposely called Himself 'the Son of Man' to indicate that such power would come within future gifts to men. He even shrunk not from including the miraculous powers also in the same inference. The joy given to a dying sinner by a priest's absolution is taken as proof of its intrinsic validity. Bishop Wordsworth, in his *Tour in Italy*, which was undertaken with the object of testing where Rome and England agreed, relates the same argument being used by a Romish priest. Carleton's well-known *Tales of Irish Peasantry* give striking instances of blindest confidence in priestly absolution, and of wildest blasphemy where a priest dared not to pronounce it. There is strong warning in Scripture against 'speaking peace when there is no peace;' and relapses from apparent sick-bed penitence are proverbial.

## Confession.

The High Church cling to the kindred Romish tenet of auricular confession to priests; though it is clear that the 'confessions' of the primitive Christian Church were only voluntary, and mutual, 'one to another,' as recommended by St. James. In our Communion Service advice is given to 'those who cannot quiet their own consciences, coming to the Lord's Table, to open their griefs to some discreet minister.' Penance is a Romish 'Sacrament;' and confession to priests is a custom in the Greek Church. Our Thirteenth Canon cautions ministers how they take confessions; and when recently five hundred Anglican priests petitioned Convocation 'for the regular licensing of confessors,' they were answered by an unanimous Resolution, which was afterwards indorsed by the whole Lambeth Conference of 1878, 'that the Twenty-fifth Article meant no such thing.' St. Augustine asks in his *Confessions*, What have I to do with men that they should hear my confessions, as if they could heal my infirmities?'

The High Church idea of Church ministry, generally,

assumes something more than the Apostle's definition, 'Servants for Christ's sake' (2 Cor. iv. 5). It would seem to trench on the vital doctrine 'There is one Mediator between God and men, the Man Christ Jesus.' But it is really only an exaggerated view of the ordained human agency. The Low Church err as much in the opposite direction. Compare their views on this subject. They have their 'Penitent Forms' almost of similar intention. But Bishop Ryle sums up his protest against High Church views on the subject in the exclamation, 'No Priest but Christ; no Confessor but Christ; no Absolver but Christ;' and of the ministry he adopts St. Paul's conception, 'We preach not ourselves, but Jesus the Lord.' He considers ministers as 'useful only so far as they promote communion between Christ and our souls, and the moment they begin to stand between the two, even in the slightest degree, they become enemies, not friends, to our peace' (p. 312).

Between these exaggerated, and depreciating, views of priestly agency no vital Christian doctrine is at stake.

## *Preaching.*

The Low Church are, however, especially addicted to running after favourite preachers who they feel to do them spiritual good, and they run after them on the strongest scent of party spirit. Each circle has its own pope, no matter to what parish he may have been assigned by ecclesiastical arrangement.

There is really no fundamental doctrine involved in the difference of views about the preaching ministry.

The liberal High Church writers of *Lux Mundi* thus reflect on Professor Milligan's words, 'Priestliness is the prime element of the Church's being.' They say, in substance, Christians as a body are a royal priesthood. Christ made them priests unto God His Father. Every Christian gives his life to God's service, and the whole Church devotes itself to the good of the whole world. Common worship requires a ministry, and the Gospel must be preached.

The teaching of the whole Church does not militate against the special order of teachers. The Apostles were as 'scribes instructed into the kingdom of heaven,' and the ministers' 'lips keep knowledge' (pp. 384, 391).

There cannot be more practical evidence of the essential unanimity of High and Low Church ministers than the perfect co-operation of missionaries sent out by the High and Low Societies, when they come together for earnest work among the heathen. While the subscribers to those societies at home are denouncing each other at home as anti-Christian, their agents are carrying out their united conflict with Antichrist, unconscious of any vital difference between them.

## High and Low Views of Church Service.

The crucial point on which to compare different views of Church Services must be the nature of the Sacraments.

To start from common ground, the Catechism defines the two Sacraments—Baptism and the Lord's Supper—as outward and visible signs of inward and spiritual grace given, ordained by Christ Himself, and generally necessary to salvation.

### *Of Baptism.*

Fairly thoughtful people, of both parties, agree that Our Lord referred to baptism when He said, 'Except a man be born again of water and of the Spirit, he cannot enter the kingdom of heaven.' High and Low views differ as to the meaning and process of new birth.

### *High Church Views.*

St. Cyril, in his allegorical manner, illustrates the higher conception of baptisms to which Our Lord raised carnal Nicodemus's curiosity, by the effect of 'water associated with fire receiving the impress of its efficacy, and so rising into higher life' (*Com. St. John*, p. 169).

Dr. Pusey thus simply puts the Church's doctrine in contrast with Calvin's: 'Justification by faith is not through feelings, but by baptism. Yet there may be a cold recognition of the gift of God by baptism without perception that by abiding faith only can that gift be retained.' In another place he gives serious warning against 'too much reliance being placed on the Ordinance independently of its effects, it being the Antinomian who supposes any justification by faith without good works accompanying.' Hooker describes the gift in baptism to be, 'a saving grace of justification, and infusion of divine virtue, giving the first disposition towards future newness of life: but,' says he, 'all do not receive the grace of God who receive this sacrament, nor is the grace of God absolutely tied to it.' Chrysostom says, 'Therefore we baptize *infants*, though they have committed no sins, that holiness may be *added* to them, and they *may become* Christ's members so grafted into Him.'

## Low Church Views.

Bishop Ryle says, 'Infants regenerated in baptism are not all made holy. Such grace can only accrue in the life.' He adds, 'Nothing in Scripture nor in Church Services supports the idea that baptism and regeneration are inseparable. Baptism is simply an Ordinance for the admission of fresh members into the Visible Church of Christ' (p. 160).

Mr. Simeon, a great Low Church authority, is quoted by Dr. Hook with commendation as 'briefly stating the truth in these words: 'The seed is sown in the heart of the baptized to grow up, and bring forth fruit; so that an infant thus brought within Christ's Church by the faith of its parents is in a state of salvation; and by the progressive renovation of its gradually awakening soul after the divine image it proves its inheritance of God's everlasting kingdom. The effectiveness of the grace, if not lost, will be seen by the fruits following.'

*Comparison.*

'All agree that regeneration *sometimes* accompanies baptism' (Hooker).

The High Church take regeneration to mean a definite gift of grace communicated in baptism, which, however, may be lost and come to nothing.

The Low Church mean by it a new condition and relation to Christ into which the infant is brought by baptism, and which may or may not be realised.

There may be still-birth in grace as well as nature. On the other hand God is able to give life without the ordinary process, even stones as children to Abraham.

The High Church untruly accuse the Low of saying that in baptism a child may, or may not, be born again; begging the question as to the meaning of the term.

The Low Church untruly accuse the High of supposing a baby to be in their sense converted in heart and character by the act of baptism.

Both High and Low believe that an infant is introduced by baptism into the household of God, the membership of Christ, and an inheritance of heaven. The gift may be forfeited says one, or never realised says the other—whether complete or inchoate is the difference between them.

Whether the baptismal gift is affected by want of faith in the parents has been decided in the negative by the Church (Bingham). Archbishop Usher says, 'The Church supposes parents bringing their offspring to baptism to be themselves believers; and so takes the infant into the Christian covenant of grace as seed of godly parents: just as in the Burial Service the Church assumes, without judging, that those whose bodies are brought for Christian burial may be 'numbered with the elect, and rest in hope of a blissful resurrection.'

Dean Church wisely takes the exaggerations of controversy as balancing opposite modes of thought: and a middle term as the true place of the Sacrament of baptism in the living system of the English Church (*Oxford Movement*, p. 228).

### The Lord's Supper.

The Twenty-eighth Article describes the Lord's Supper as 'not only a sign of the love that Christians ought to have among themselves, but a Sacrament of our redemption by Christ's death, which rightly received with faith is a partaking of the Body and Blood of Christ, . . . but only after a heavenly and spiritual manner.'

The word 'only' in this Article was matter of debate. Our Lord, however, was very express in explaining to His Disciples, who found it hard to believe that they were eating His Flesh, and drinking His Blood, in His Presence, at the institution of the Sacrament, that His words, 'This is My Body, this is My Blood,' were spirit, and that the flesh profited nothing. No doubt the Romish priests have found, and still find, the supposition of their miraculous function of transubstantiation very profitable to their influence. But Paul was content to say, 'Though we have known Christ after the flesh, yet now know we Him so no more.'

It is in the literal or figurative acceptation of these words that the difference of views of High and Low Church on this subject consists.

It was lately argued by a correspondent with the *Guardian* that the copula must be taken to unite two identical things. That Our Lord could not have used so graphic an expression as 'This Bread is My Flesh' figuratively. In this view, when Paul said of the parallel Jewish Sacrament, 'This Rock was Christ,' he affirmed a literal transubstantiation of the source of their spiritual drinking (1 Cor. x. 4). The same rule of interpretation would make the inspired words 'Hagar was Mount Sinai' imply Ishmael's birth from a mountain (Gal. iv. 25). St. Paul followed up Our Saviour's words about the Sacrament by the inference that communicants themselves *are one bread*, being partakers of the one Bread.

Our Lord made constant use of parable in teaching: 'Without a parable spake He not.' He knew how strongly the *oculis subjecta* affect the human heart by their outward illustration of hidden truths, and give sensible help to faith. 'He knows how little we are able to realise heavenly and spiritual things unseen, and pities our feeble apprehension' (Bishop Ken).

Not till the ninth century was the doctrine of literal transubstantiation promulgated in the Romish Church. Paschasius is said by Bellarmine to have been the first to assert categorically that 'the consecrated bread was the actual and same Body which was born of Mary.' This he maintained in an argument against Bertram, who had quoted the expression of St. Ambrose, 'not physical verity, but spiritual mystery.' At the Fourth Vatican Council, in the tenth century, Innocent the Third made literal transubstantiation a Church dogma. Bossuet offered this apology: 'pour ôter l'horreur de manger sa chair, et de boire son sang, il les donnait enveloppés sous une espèce étrangère.'

No wonder our Twenty-eighth Article discards such fancies as 'superstition, repugnant to the words of Scripture, and overthrowing the nature of a sacrament.'

The Romish Mass was plainly called by Cardinal Bona 'the bloodless immolation;' and such meaning was as plainly condemned by Cranmer as 'vainly treating the bread which you hold in your hand as part of the Body sacrificed.' Lightfoot cries out, 'No more victims, no more priests offering sacrifices to make atonement!' The corporeal presence of the Host is an idea utterly discarded in our Church.

## High Church Views.

The objectivity of High Church ideas naturally clings to the actual conversion of the bread and wine in some sense into the very Body and Blood of Our Lord; and a compromise, between the literal and figurative meaning of Our Lord's words, is found in the phrase 'Real Presence.' It did not require the reams that have been written to show that this phrase bears either meaning, according to the sense in which the word 'Real' is taken. 'Real,' in the sense of *substantial* (as in the phrase real property), would qualify the Presence as corporeally in the bread; but in the sense of *actual* it might imply no more than a very special Presence of Christ 'in the midst, where two or three are so solemnly gathered together in His name.' A definition by an equivocal term is valueless, or mischievous as a deceit to those who use it, and to those who hear it used. Such a disputant as Mr. Enraght could stand firm to the literal meaning, and yet suppose it to imply a Spiritual eating of the Flesh, taking the metaphor and the fact as one idea. An actual divine communication all agree to—'a dwelling in Christ, and Christ in us.' Cranmer meant plainly transubstantiation by Real Presence, when he prosecuted those who rejected the term; and he afterwards died for rejecting it in that sense himself. Dr. Harrison's 'Answer to Dr. Pusey's Challenge' on the contrary as plainly maintains that wherever the word Presence is used by any of the Fathers in relation to the Eucharist, Christ's *spiritual*, not *corporeal*, is meant.'

The phrase 'Real Presence' is supposed by many to reconcile the objective and subjective views. Bishop Ridley died rather than take the cover of equivocation; but he pointed out that the partaking of Christ all profess, only differing in the *manner*; whether it be meant a partaking of His Passion, or the grosser idea of the Body itself. The fact is, our Prayer-Book has so much of the same language as the Missal, care being taken to avoid unnecessary difference suggesting distinctive doctrine. Jeremy Taylor, in a large spirit of Christian peace, says: 'Enter not into curious inquiries, and differing apprehensions of mysteriousness or seemingly opposed doctrines, by which good men stand at a distance, and are afraid of each other. Since all societies of Christians pretend to the greatest esteem of this the holiest of all the ministries of religion. All speak honourable things of it, and suppose great blessings from it.' On 'Real Presence' (edit. 1865, p. 13), he asks, 'Where is the intelligible difference between Christ's Body being present in the Sacrament *really but spiritually*, and in the Romish view *substantially but mysteriously as a spirit?*' And (p. 28), 'Rome and England may be reconciled by explanation of the terms used.' And so may High and Low agree to the phrase 'Real Presence' between the two senses of the word 'Real,' as *substantial* or *actual*.

Dr. Pusey says: 'The dispute between Rome and England is as to any change of substance.' In his *Eirenicon* he replies to Cardinal Manning's allegation of English disbelief in transubstantiation and the sacrifice of the Mass, by saying, '*We* do believe a real objective presence of Christ's Body and Blood; but in a spiritual manner.'

Alexander Knox described himself as 'though in sentiment far from High Church, yet finding many points of agreement' (i. 392, 5th edit., 1844). 'The Eucharistic symbols, when once sanctified according to the Lord's appointment, become, in an inexplicable but deeply awful manner, the receptacles of that heavenly virtue which His divine power qualifies them to convey. Christ consecrated bread and wine the virtual representations of His Body and Blood in this Sacrament; and, by consequence, the effective vehicles of their influence to all capable partakers.' He thought the English Church the destined link between objective and subjective views; and the difference between a *spiritual bodily* presence and a *bodily spiritual* presence to consist of a refinement of idea evanescent to plain practical apprehension. The pervading idea of Canon Paget's essay in *Lux Mundi* is that the consecration of material elements to be the vehicles of Divine grace keeps up that vindication of the material against sham spiritualism which the Incarnation and Ascension of Jesus Christ achieved; and so Christianity maintains its hold on the whole life of man. Means appealing to the senses effect the work of God on the soul.

## Low Church Views.

Bishop Ryle thus expounds the Low Church view (p. 239) in brief: 'There is a real spiritual presence of Christ with true communicants in the Lord's Supper. That great ordinance of Christ has a special blessing in His peculiar presence to the heart of believing communicants. The words, "Take, eat," mean that believers eating that bread in remembrance of Christ find a special presence of Christ in their hearts, and a special revelation of His sacrifice of His Body and Blood in their souls. His bodily presence they cannot find either personally, or in the representative signs consecrated.' He refers to the Rubric at the end of the Communion Service, by which it is declared that no adoration ought to be made either to the sacramental bread and wine, or unto any corporal presence of Christ's natural flesh and blood (p. 249).

## Reflections.

Strange indeed it is that the most sacred means ordained for all men's peace with God, and with each other should offer the greatest bone of contention. It was immediately after the institution of this Sacrament that Our Lord gave, in its illustration, the Parable of the Vine. The grafting into Himself, and of all into one Body, as the branches united to a vine-stem, represents a communion of far deeper meaning than can be affected by any difference of view as to its process. Those who can lose such union of heart and soul with the Lord and with each other, in dispute about the means, are not worthy communicants themselves. They are unduly troubled with rufflings on the surface of a transcendent depth of peace. The 'Sacramentum Eucharistiæ' of our Latin Article is what we ask God to accept at the conclusion of the Office —'our sacrifice of praise and thanksgiving.' The High Church prefer calling it a celebration, the Low a communion, both being Prayer-Book phrases, but respectively significant of the objective and subjective view of the same great service. How can Bishop Ryle say that great principles are at stake ? (p. 221.) Considering even the extreme of superstition in one direction, and the coldest rejection of all mystery in the other, all may unite in full communion with Our Lord, and with each other, while contemplating the Sacred Body and Blood however really, or only emblematically, presented to their joint devotion.

*Fasting Communion.*

The High Church attach much importance to a precedence of the Lord's Supper before the taking of any common food.

A view so materialistic seems in strange contrast with higher conceptions of the sacred ordinance. But it naturally belongs to objective apprehension, identifying the symbols with the worship itself. Surely reverence is misplaced when consecrated elements are ranked in any order of precedence with common food. A tract much used on the subject relates that a Bishop of Alexandria in the fourth century raised serious questions whether a man into whose mouth a splash of water from his bath had entered was fit to communicate that day. So fanciful may arbitrary notions of the most sacred subjects become. The most rigid fasters allow themselves a cup of tea, which is worse than a splash of water. Fasting Communion, however, is said to have been a custom of the Church; and therefore, as *mos pro lege*, an unwritten law. But Augustine, who is the chief referee for what is called custom of the Church, expressly states that this custom was caused by the irregularities in 'Love Feasts,' referred to in the epistle to the Corinthians, from which it became necessary to separate Communions.

The first institution was 'after supper,' for which, however, Gregory Nazianzen apologises, saying, 'Every action of Our Lord is not necessary to be imitated, and there is no command that the details of Maundy Thursday, on which day the first institution is followed exactly, should be considered a pattern for all celebrations.'

The first 'breaking of bread,' after the Resurrection, by Christ Himself with the disciples at Emmaus, was 'as they were eating,' and St. Paul's after his sermon at Troas was near midnight.

It is alleged that there is practical advantage in communicating the first thing at daybreak, before the thoughts are dissipated by breakfast conversation; but there is no necessity for such discomposure, and the mind may be both more vigorous and more collected, by preparation for later communion, to which the morning service also will lead up. A hurried rush from bed precludes any immediately preceding preparation, and is an effort tending to relax attention to subsequent devotions through the day, as is obviously the case in the habits of foreign Sundays. But the Creator hallowed the whole seventh day as not too much refreshment of the higher spirit for making religion of all the week's employment.

## On Fasting in general.

Our Rubric assigns a third of every year for days of abstinence. Forty days in Lent, Fridays, Ember Days, Vigils, etc., exceed altogether a hundred days.

The High Church think more of such observances as being appointed by the Church. The Low Church think more abstractedly of the benefit derived by both from such observances.

The Lenten fast of forty days is a part of the course adopted by Christians of seasons commemorative of the events of Our Lord's life on earth. Every spring the miraculous discipline He underwent in preparation for His opening ministry, and for His crucial conflict with the Prince of this world, is sympathetically commemorated. No actual imitation every year of this superhuman action could, of course, have been imagined; but a specially penitential season was set apart commemoratively, and for the cultivation of the same spirit of humiliation and discipline.

All religions have fasting seasons. The Mohammedan Ramadhan exactly coincides with the Christian Lent.

The fasts related in the Old Testament are chiefly connected with special occasions, both private and public, but there were also appointed seasons when 'the bread of affliction' was eaten (Deut. vi.). Whether stated fasts, or fasts on occasions of special undertakings, distresses, sorrows, or penitencies, all meant prostration of the soul before God, in confession and supplication.

There are no specific rules in Scripture for modes of fasting—there is not even a direct command to fast; but the habitual practice is assumed; and when Our Lord was asked why His disciples fasted not, He replied that they would do so when He was no longer visibly with them. He said, indeed, on one occasion that an unclean spirit could only be got rid of by prayer and fasting. His only direction on the subject was that none should fast for merit or ostentation, for the reward was higher in secret and with God. In the Old Testament true fasting is expressly distinguished form 'bowing down the head like a bulrush,' and associated with active service and self-sacrifice, 'loosing the bonds of wickedness, and letting the oppressed go free' (Isaiah lviii. 5.)

Neither in the Old nor New Dispensation has fasting any Scriptural authority in the sense of asceticism, which was never entertained as doctrine in the Church at all till the second century, though dating far back in Eastern practice. The word itself is a Greek expression for severe athletic training, which St. Paul compared with Christian discipline to shame its comparative laxity, though in a higher sense and aim. Asceticism, in the idea of self-infliction, was a doctrine of Pythagoras, and of Stoic philosophy, and gave a name to a contemporary sect of Jews. It crept into the Church with Monasticism, and going into a convent became synonymous with entering religious life. The genial spirit of Christianity has little sympathy with the narrow cliqueship of unsocial reclusion, nor its diffuse enjoyment with the singularity of bodily austerities and abstinence.

Fasting, in the grosser sense of deprivation of ordinary sustenance for full capacity of active service, cannot be such as the Rubric means for practice during a third of every year. That were a contradiction of all Scripture and common sense.

The Romish Church, enjoining fasts in number more than those we have retained, loses all sight of the working—that is, the most numerous—classes; and has led the wealthier classes to sham pretences of fasting by gastronomic distinctions of more delicate feeding.

A man in health should, ordinarily, eat and drink no more than he wants for active life. To eat less resembles what is called in the army *malingering*, which is a sham disabling. To eat habitually more than nature needs, for pleasure, is what Scripture calls idolatry of the belly. There are festive occasions when more befits, for mental stimulant and social enjoyment, as Our Lord's first miracle 'showed forth.' There are, also, seasons of depression, or voluntary subjection of animal spirits, and retirement for reflection and spiritual exercise, for which less food is suitable. David on one such season said he forgot to eat his bread, which Dr. Johnson declared he had never known any man's grief to amount to.

It may be thought as most men do not ordinarily restrict what they eat and drink to only what they want for strength, these observations are not of general application. But rules are not meant to meet excess. The Scripture rule is that 'every creature of God is to be received with thanksgiving, and nothing to be refused,' but all temperately used (1 Tim. iv. 4). Temperate feeders can but adapt this lowest feature of fasting discipline to its purpose.

The High Church take the Table of Fasts as formal rules for imperative observance.

The Low Church follow their own judgment in the use of Church appointments, and quote St. Paul against fasting as a formal observance, ' Let the heart be established with grace; and not with meats, which have not profited them that have been occupied therein ' (Heb. xiii. 9).

No doctrine is at stake in such matters of discipline.

## Saints' Days.

The High Church naturally attach more authority than the Low to holy days, which are appointments of the Church. Indeed they rank some of them on a par with the day divinely hallowed from the Creation for the spiritual necessities and blessing of mankind. This primeval institution of the Sabbath, now the Christian Sunday, 'remembered' in the commandments, and promised a blessing throughout Scripture, 'poured out from heaven such that there shall not be room to receive it,' is the breathing time of man's spiritual life. 'Holy days' are valuable means adopted by the Church for impressing on men's minds the most important features of Gospel history. They were, in fact, an adaptation by the Church of previous sacred habits, embraced and consecrated by Christianity. As synagogues, and afterward temples, were purposely engaged as the first churches, and the vestments of heathenism were interwoven with the paraphernalia of true religion, so the *feriæ* and *dies festi* were enlisted as Christian holidays, to be kept specially apart from *dies profesti*, in honour of great events and persons.

The first Christian Saints' Day memoralised the martyrdom of Ignatius and Polycarp. Others rapidly followed; and, as churches multiplied, like honour was done by each to local saints, and Rome asserted her pretensions to supremacy by adopting them all into her Calendar. The number became excessive, and a rivalry of honours began, sometimes given unworthily, and from interest, causing scandal.

Our Church at the Reformation retained only a few of these days for special memory of Our Lord, The Virgin Mother, the Apostles, and the first Martyr.

Invocation of Saints was an abuse growing out of this practice, severely condemned in our Twenty-second Article as repugnant to Scripture and superstitious.

The mind finds natural relief, from the mental strain of worshipping the Invisible, by a resort to more intelligible objects. Hence Romish Mariolatry, pilgrimages, sacred shrines, and relics. Mr. Gladstone defended the remarkable essay *Ecce Homo*, from the charge that it laid too much stress on Our Lord's humanity, on this very ground, 'that a yearning for human aid is caused by insufficient realisation of the fact that we possess it fully in Christ Himself.' The lowest conception needs help for spiritual elevation, and the highest not to lose Christ's reflection in forms of hagiolatry. Saints' days are valued by both High and Low Church in different views—the one more highly appreciating them as authoritative ordinances, the other as felt by them to be useful, but by both as cultivators of sacred memories so realised in the heart.

We all keep anniversaries of events and persons associated with, and embodied in, our affections, some as institutions, others of our own choice. The observance of Saints' Days fortifies our common belief in 'the Communion of Saints,' and in the identity of the Church through all its vicissitudes.

High Church accuse the Low of depreciating sacred appeals of this kind; Low Church accuse the High of idolatry in the observance.

The Puritans of Cromwell's army took more offence at window-paintings, and statues representing the Virgin and Child, than at any other so-called vestige of Popery, and their iconoclastic fury was more directed against memorials of Saints than any other feature of their rejected modes of worship.

We can now more calmly recognise the possible union between objective love of representation, and subjective sublimation of idea, in joint observance of set holy days.

## Ritual.

It is a noble idea, specially of the High Church, that the worship of God should enlist the best of all our faculties and powers, as the fullest offering possible of the whole man, and the utmost exercise of his reason, taste, and imagination in address to Him Who will be 'loved with all the heart, mind, soul, and strength.' 'All the external gifts of art, such as architecture, painting, and music, may be consecrated to worship' (*Lux Mundi*, p. 392).

The Low Church are less demonstrative; or, as they could say of themselves, less theatrical in their propensities.

The worship of the heart may be the same from both natures, which differ in themselves, and not in their intention.

The High Church make appeal to the senses of sight and sound to arouse devotion ; *to the eye* by dramatic scenery, vestures, processions with flags and banners, illuminations, pictures, images, gesticulations, postures, crossings, and the screened-off stage [1] for the professional performers, the

---

[1] No doubt the idea is that only priests, and their acolytes, should enter the holiest place.

audience rising as they come on; *to the ear* by elaborately artistic music, with loud instruments reducing prayer to *obbligato*; the service recitative in formal monotone, stript of natural expression.

The less dramatic Low Church find such appeals to the senses a hindrance rather than a help to their devotion, and assume a plain simplicity, exaggerated in opposition; prayers of individual accentuation; psalmody through the nose, or read like prose; and endless preaching.

A man may, indeed, be so engrossed by the devotion, and absorbed in the address to present Deity as to be almost unconscious of any peculiarity in the mode of worship; but the two contrasted modes are distinctly characteristic of the objective and subjective natures of men's minds.

It is folly to attach any notion of superiority to the ornate kind of worship, or to assert for the plain worship exclusive spirituality. The majority of any congregation may well be allowed to have their own way, with decent Christian care not needlessly to offend what they think the prejudices of the rest.

In Papal countries, and in English High Church sometimes, worship is made purposely attractive as scenic oratorio, sometimes with admission by tickets.

The Spanish invaders of the New World found a splendid ritual the most effective means of wholesale proselytising. A grand spectacle gains the easiest access to uncultured minds. The Romish missionaries have always had an advantage over our less dramatic agents among the heathen. Henry Martyn, with his matchless zeal of piety, made no such conquests for the English Church in India as Huc in Tartary for the Jesuits.

The senses may be good conductors to the heart. The senses give the first impressions. But there is danger in dwelling too much in the sphere of sense. Spiritual life finds its sustenance after first apprehension in the region of the will. The great probation of life is the passage through outward objects in this world to inward fitness for the next. In any other idea present interests are disconnected from their intended results.

Some are more sensitive than others to the influence of the senses, others arrive at truths more naturally by inward experiences. High and Low Church might be distinguished as the one feeling by seeing, the other seeing by feeling. Metaphysicians discriminate the two modes of apprehension as presentative and intuitive, and the same idea embraced either way may give equally and similarly actuating motive. In the matter of ritualism the apparatus of worship has its only value in kindling devotion to the glory of God. Bishop Ryle truly warns that 'our minds are too ready to turn away from spiritual to visible things,' but he too indiscriminately denounces visible ceremonial as defeating the very purpose of worship' (p. 353).

Queen Elizabeth, before any actual schism had begun, commanded fifty-three 'Articles of Dispensation' to be read in churches every quarter of a year, by which she hoped to enforce uniformity in mode of worship; and 'all sort of operatic performance' to be so limited as, in Neal's estimation, should have satisfied the Puritans. Prayers were 'only to be *sung* in Collegiate Churches, and *there* so as to be understood by common people. For the comfort of such as delight in music a hymn, and such like song might be permitted at the end of common prayer.' Neal adds that 'the Puritan disputes, beginning about vestments, organs, cross in baptism, and such like things, gradually caused misgivings, on both sides, that they were fighting about trifles. Pious persons lamented, atheists laughed, and Papists blew the coals' (*Hist.* iv. 105).

That the different estimates of ritual result from difference of mental constitution is evident from the certainty that no man of exquisite taste for music, or of theatrical fancy, or of pictorial imagination could take Low Church views of worship; nor, on the other hand, could any man insensible to music, immovable by drama, untouched by traits of beauty, find his prosaic nature rise to High Church elevation. There are men of high intellect and principle who have failed even to entertain without contempt the questions raised in late disputes about ritual. Dean Stanley ridiculed in Convocation the disturbance of the Church 'about clergymen's clothes.'

Ritual is the manual of order and forms to be observed in Divine Service. Its obvious use and necessity is for decency, and, as far as possible, uniformity, in Christian worship, instead of one setting up something different from others. It is absurd to suppose vital doctrine involved in its greater or less appreciation. There is no orthodoxy in appeal to the senses, nor heterodoxy in 'Praise God Barebones;' though there is incompleteness in any worship which does not 'glorify God in our bodies and in our spirits which are His' (1 Cor. vi. 20). In that view the two ideas of worship could unite more thoroughly in what is essential to both!

## The Lincoln Judgment.

Disputes about rites and ceremonies have lately received a judgment from the Primate, Benson, of the highest order, both of judicial acumen, and conciliatory Christian spirit.

The questions seemed scarcely worthy of such elaborate treatment—*haud dignus vindice nodus.*

A Low Church Association arraigned a High Church Prelate, of great estimation, for practices alleged to be inconsistent with the legal construction of the Rubric as amended at the Reformation.

### *Mixed Chalice.*

The first point referred for decision was the authority for mixing water with Sacramental wine.

A rubric retained in the Prayer-Book of 1549 showed

that this practice was recognised then, but the omission of words in the next edition implied a cessation of the mixing during the actual service, though it seems to have continued to be done before the service began. The judgment was given 'that the mixture, as part of the service, is against the law, but the use of a cup mixed beforehand is not an ecclesiastical offence.' *Risum teneatis?*

The practice could only have any value symbolically, and even *that* in very various senses, at different times. It is stated, in this judgment, that 'in the third century the mixture of water with the wine was taken to represent the union of Christ with His Disciples; but that three principal Liturgies connect it with the effusion from Our Lord's side of water and blood; and the Romish Church generally attached to it a signification of Christ's union of humanity and divinity.' Some consider it symbolical of the connection between both the Sacraments; but that idea might suggest a parallel mixture of wine with the water of baptism! The libations of classic ritual were usually mixed; the thick wine of olden time requiring dilution. The mixed chalice was sometimes defended in a 'temperance' view, taken from the excesses to which the Love Feasts became liable; but this view received authoritative condemnation.

Dr. Hook (*Ch. Dict.* p. 801) observes that 'in the ancient Church the people brought offerings of bread and wine to the priests, from which the Sacramental elements were taken;' and Cardinal Bona relates that 'when such contribution ceased, the clergy having to provide the elements themselves invented symbolisms of their own, both in way of mixing the wine, and substituting unleavened wafers for the broken bread.' St. Chrysostom (*Comm. Matth.* xxvi. 29) objects to any 'departure from the plain description given by Our Lord of the "fruit of the vine."' Surely High and Low may agree in the Primate's conclusion that such embellishments of the Divine ordinance cannot be of any authority or sufficient importance to be thrust on unsympathetic congregations.' Irenæus interpreted the words of Isaiah (l. 22), 'Thy vintners mingle wine and water,' to mean that 'the elders mingled with the plain institutions of God their own diluting traditions.'

## Candles.

One of the points submitted for judgment was the authority for lighting candles on the altar by daylight.

This practice was expressly limited, by an Injunction of Edward VI., to 'the lighting of two candles only on the high altar;' and this was said to be meant to symbolise Christ as the Light of the World. Our Lord, in His common way of parable-teaching, made a like symbolical application to Himself of the light from the Candelabrum in the Temple.

A great accumulation of argument and learning was collected in the judgment about this use of candles. Very harmless, one would think it, if it helps any one's devotion without disturbing others. But the Romish Church has made such an abuse of the lighting, and carrying about of candles, as a business very subservient to priestly emolument; and so mystified the meaning, whether for use or ornament, that one wonders less at the dispute being raised. The Low Church, sniffing Popery in the practice, stand up for the strict letter of the Statute; and even argue that its restraint on the practice altogether must be absolute, as we have now no 'high altar.' But Dr. Hook replies, 'that it is the high altar alone that remains in our churches,' all the rest having been condemned on account of the idolatrous practices that were connected with them.' The High Church, however, are setting up little side altars again; and they evade King Edward's Statute, about allowing 'only two candles' by putting more upon adjoining ledges on the wall.

The disputation is unworthy of Sacramental connection altogether, both in its matter and manner, on both sides.

Bingham thus quotes St. Jerome on the subject (ii. 461), 'Candles being lighted by day as well as night was an innovation on an old custom, which grew from the Christians secretly assembling in hiding places for fear of persecution.' The Council of Eliberis condemned lights in daytime, 'lest they might molest the spirits of the saints.' But St. Jerome relates that 'in all the churches in the East, when the Gospel is about to be preached, lights were kindled though the sun was shining bright; to show a sign of rejoicing.' To some minds a blaze of candles may seem to do honour to Divine service. Dr. Ryle, however, thinks such illumination 'spoils the dignity and simplicity of New Testament worship' (p. 353).

The Primate's Pastoral, following his judgment, calls attention to the ruling principle of St. Paul's life and counsel, that not all that is lawful is expedient, and urges considerateness towards even over-sensitive or prejudiced fellow-Christians. This good advice may check High Church contempt of conscientious photophobia, and mitigate Low Church fretting at the legal limit of two candles if not surreptitiously exceeded on adjoining ledges.

Certainly no vital doctrine can be involved in a taste or distaste for illumination, but the supposed honour should be offered, if at all, to God, and not to Saints, or Virgin Mother.

## *Eastward Position.*

The Primate had also to pronounce judgment as to the right place in which the celebrant should stand during parts of the Communion Service. The malpractice alleged was standing on the west side of the Holy Table, and not at the north end.

Ever since Laud's time Puritan objection has been taken to the officiating minister so standing, and facing eastward while consecrating the elements, for the reason assigned that he so hides what he is doing from the sight of the congregation. The various positions of the table itself at various times make the terms of Rubrics on the subject indefinite, much depending on which is the end or side. The judgment dismisses the question as immaterial, and devoid of all doctrinal interest; as 'the imputed sacrificial significance of the facing eastward is new and forced, and can have no effect in rendering the position either desirable on the one side, or illegal on the other.' When the table is so placed that the minister, facing eastward, might screen his mode of action, one would wish the congregation better occupied than in attempts to see.

### *Agnus Dei.*

Singing the Anthem 'O Lamb of God' just after the Prayer of Consecration was another point referred to judgment. It offends the Low Church, as associated with the Mass, and adoration of the Host, and implying an actual though unbloody sacrifice, perpetuated by priests, of the Divine Victim once offered for us all.

But the words 'O Lamb of God' occur in parts of the Communion Service where they can have no such meaning.

The Primate judged that the Agnus Anthem at the moment of consecration was inexpedient, but not illegal.

### *General Reflection.*

In deference to the Primate's authority both High and Low Church may well agree to differ within the range he liberally, and considerately, allows as involving no essential doctrine in dispute, or rubrical illegality.

Mr. Gladstone well remarked in the debate on the 'Public Worship Bill,' when it was avowedly introduced to proscribe ritualism, that 'the lapse of time since the Rubrics' last correction, the multitude of particulars, the doubts of interpretation, and diversities of custom, make it unreasonable to restrain varieties of opinion and usage.' 'The Church could not be preserved if we shift its balance of doctrinal expression, or if we treat rubrical interpretation as the basis of doctrinal significance.' If litigation be unavoidable, 'it should be confined to the testing of such proceedings as imply unfaithfulness to the national religion.'

The Judicial Committee of the Privy Council have dismissed an appeal against the Primate's judgment. The country may be congratulated on a practical termination of Church conflict on such questions, evidently beyond even Lord Grimthorpe's power of resuscitation.

This judgment cannot be considered a victory for High or Low, but it is a final judicial decision, in Christian spirit, for mutual toleration, on points of exaggerated disputation of secondary importance, disturbing the Church, and the delight of scoffers.

Neutrality can scarcely be hoped for where parties have so long hoisted hostile flags of doctrinal symbolism: but the opponents may become conscious of disproportionate zeal in the cause, and may find better scope for their energies in joint defence of interests common to both.

The prosecuted Bishop, and those sympathising with him, have announced full submission to the judgment now confirmed; but, it may be hoped, they have done so more candidly than a Bishop who has communicated to the *Guardian* his appreciation of the *Eirenicon* as a triumph to be meekly taken on his side, and as an opportunity for the other's to drop all he dislikes. Rather let those rejoice who find aid to their devotion in the utmost permitted ritualism, and let those whom Lord Grimthorpe describes as 'neither ordered by the judgment to do anything they have not done, nor to abstain from anything they have done,' be content to cease strife on such comfortable terms.

'Common Prayer' is the object, and the priceless jewel of peace and love, in the act of making such an offering to the God of love, must not be lost in disputes about its setting.

Bishop Alford exaggerates ritualistic hostility so far as to suppose joint communion impossible. It may be hoped he stands almost alone in such a view. Lord Grimthorpe only exhibits the result of long exacerbated controversy to the extent of confounding what we still hold in common with Rome with what the Reformation delivered us from. He supposes anything practised or believed in Rome must be antagonistic to our Reformation, and wicked. He condemns all 'pre-reformation practices' as part of the errors reformed. He believes a reformed Church can retain nothing of its former self. He argues that any ritualism which existed before the Reformation is only retained in England for love of the corruptions of Rome. The High Church take the retention of old practices, so far as they are sound, as the best part of the Reformation, and approve the recent judgment expressly for its recognition of primitive connection. Of course the day-lit candles, Eastward position, and Agnus-singing may be used by some to express the Romish idea of the Mass: but so may anti-ritualists pervert, in their way, Church regulation to wrong meaning. Both ways the true meaning of our Church is departed from. It is truly remarked in the very sensible *Spectator* that the tendency of the Lincoln Judgment is to make High and Low Church see that on the very secondary subject of ritual there are no differences between them to prevent their cordially communicating together.

## The Difference of High and Low Church Views, though not Vital, are not Unimportant.

The different aspects in which religious worship presents itself to the two main classes of minds may be partially distinguished by the descriptions mutually given of them by historical writers of both classes, and especially by writers at crucial periods of contest or transition.

Macaulay characterised the High Church as a worship of ecclesiastical government. Hallam called it a special attachment to hierarchy.

Dean Church, in the *Oxford Movement*, says of Whately and Arnold, as the precursors of that High Church revival, 'they could not open their Prayer-Books without seeing that, on the face of it, the Church claimed to be something very different from what it was assumed to be in the current controversies of the time' (p. 7). He described the previous Evangelical revival as 'recommending itself by gifts of flowing words, not unfruitful of zeal and of philanthropy; but never seeming to get beyond the first beginning of Christian teaching—the call to repentance, and assurance of forgiveness. It had nothing to say to the process of building up the new life. It had consecrated phrases, claiming exclusive spirituality and unworldliness.'

Aubrey Moore, one of the best of what may be called the free High Church writers of *Lux Mundi*, exhibits the link between the moderate of both views. He says: 'If the sacrificial system loses its true significance in the recognition of the holiness of God and sinfulness of man, and becomes ritual, perfunctory, and formal, it is hateful to God. Not sacrifice but holiness, not external works but inward faith, not deeds of the law but the righteousness which is of God, is what He requires' (p. 73). And further (p. 74), 'Every protest against formalism and unreality in religion, and every attack on ecclesiasticism and priestcraft, owes its strength to the truth that, in the Christian idea, religion and morals are inseparably united.'

Thus both views coalesce in mutual supplement to each other.

Lightfoot rejoiced in the width of St. Paul's loving comprehension when he addressed the Philippians as 'all partakers of his grace,' including the Judaising formalists with the more spiritual Christians; and exhorting them all to strive together in the faith of the Gospel.

Vital doctrine is not necessarily implicated in the distinction between High and Low Church. Christian faith is matter transcendent to the mode of accepting it. Even idolatry of forms and means on one side, and the most slovenly negligence of rules, and self-direction by inward impulse, on the other, may not, even in their extremes, be more than diseases of true Church membership. Still they are diseases which *may* be symptomatic of unsoundness, and which must be productive of very seriously ill effects on Christian spirit.

The devotees of ceremony who expect virtue *ex opere operato*, and look to human ministry for direct mediation with God, and the careless invokers of the Spirit's response to their unaided call, are both in danger.

Each wants what the other indulges in excess. Both live in peril of self-complacency and contempt of those '-who are not as they are.' Pharisaism and schism are equal tendencies either way.

Even though modes of apprehension may only differ objectively and subjectively, or as poetic and prosaic faculties, yet human pugnacity will breed antagonism out of every difference, and in these matters antagonism is destructive of the spirit, which is on both sides equally essential.

So, though the difference between High and Low Church may not be vital, it is of grave importance in its effects.

### Fundamental Christian doctrine is held in common.

William Palmer opens his fifth chapter on *The Church* with these words, 'That Our Lord, in the time of His sojourn on earth, and afterwards by His Apostles, made a revelation of truths necessary to be believed, is the general confession of all Christians.'

All doctrine which may be fairly called *fundamental* must be believed by every Christian. All that the universal Church teaches must be matter of faith, as distinguished from matter of judgment or opinion, on which latter (said St. Augustine), 'there may be disagreement while the union of faith is preserved.' Our Church enunciates essential doctrine in Creeds and Articles, a denial or explaining away of any of which by any individual must amount to self-excommunication from our Church.

But false doctrine, and wrong notions of administration, are very distinguishable kinds of error.

Heresy is a deliberate rejection of established doctrine; and all errors, even in matter of faith, are not heresies. Much error may be venial from early inculcation and circumstances.

Lord Grimthorpe, addressing the Protestant Church Alliance (January 1889), challenged the High Church to name any doctrine they did not hold in common with Rome, excepting only Papal Supremacy, Infallibility, and the Immaculate Conception. He might have added Purgatory, though some Anglican writers are coquetting with this doctrine in theories about everlasting punishment, and further probation after death. But Lord Grimthorpe is a type of those who have been so blinded with the dust of controversy as not to see that what our Church protested against was not the great truths we must hold in common with Rome, but the errors, corruptions, and assumptions of the Papacy. The struggle of the Reformation so confused men's minds as to identify the Church of Rome with those errors instead of distinguishing them. This reminds one of Lord Raglan, when in joint command with St. Arnaud in the Crimea, old and long continued warfare having identified the relation of French and English with national hostility, frequently forgetting himself in discussing different views with his colleague, and calling his allies 'the enemy.'

It is this sort of confusion that leads many to talk of the Reformation as having introduced a new religion—new faith—new church—into England.

There is no difference between High and Low Churchmen on such vital doctrines as the Incarnation, Atonement, Resurrection of Our Lord, or the Inspiration of Scripture.

On all such points they are mainly agreed. Bishop Ryle stigmatises all High Church as Romanists, and Mr. Compton, in a recent essay, stamps all Low Church in common as Puritans. Such a cynic as Charles Greville sneers at the vulgar preaching of Spurgeon as 'dragging down the Church to Puritanical level, and stripping it of all its splendour' (vol. ii. p. 88). But our Church is not so divided, as between Romanist and Puritan, in two separate camps. The largest part of doctrinal ground is occupied in common by Rome, High and Low Church, and Dissenters too. During the Oxford controversies the 'Martyrs' Memorial' was devised for a test of orthodoxy, according to the giving or refusing of subscriptions to its erection. But the test failed to distinguish the loyal from the disloyal. Dr. Pusey subscribed, and Newman refused, and there was the same indiscriminate mixture among the Low Church.

The 'ideal churchman,' Ward, candidly confessed that 'the Evangelicals and Anglicans were equally obliged to have recourse to explanations which, to all but themselves, were unintelligible and unsatisfactory' (*Oxford Movement*, p. 193).

High and Low Church have found their dispute very indefinite. Their strifes of late have greatly served to discover that common ground which has been only viewed by each in different aspects.

It is disputed that difference of mental constitution cannot account for the difference between High and Low

Church views, because then all High Churchmen would take entirely one view, and Low Churchmen the other. But there is no such rigid line to be drawn between the two. The same mind is differently affected by the same thing in different moods or circumstances. Minds also of naturally opposite tendencies sometimes interchange their characteristics. Liddon, Keble, Pusey, though High Church leaders, were deeply spiritually-minded; and cared less for outward ceremonial than generally characterises High Churchmen. On the other hand, nothing is so theatrical as the spirituality of the ultra-Low Church—rivalling, and competing with, that of the Salvation Army.

High and Low Church are nearer each other *au fond* than they think, and share each other's defects as well as merits. A man may curse the Pope, and set himself up as pope in his own circle. Another may denounce schism, and assert for himself exclusive churchmanship. In the healthiest action of each propensity there is no rigidly dividing line between them; nor any monopoly of speciality in either.

## The difference of High and Low Church Views is inseparable from human nature.

If it be true that there are two main diversities of mental constitution which naturally estimate all matters of interest differently, either in favour of established habit or according to apparent utility, of course the matter of highest interest cannot escape this distinction of treatment.

The interest of endless consequences must dwarf all temporal interests, which, indeed, are only incidental or auxiliary to it. All know there is a *via sola salutis*, but men will differently treat its accompaniments, according to their nature. The clingers to the Ark, and the searchers-out for traces of the promised shore, all looked to the Ark, whether dwelling or returning to it, till the tokens of its rest were secure.

The Bishop of Calcutta relates that amongst the Christianised Brahmins the same distinction is apparent, of High and Low Church aspect, as amongst Christians at home. Though brought up in the same school, having studied the same books, and in every way lived under the same influences, they evince the same duality of mental disposition in different embracement of the faith which is common among men on every subject.

In fact the absence anywhere of such natural diversity would be a symptom of want of freedom and vitality; and, in the Church, a defect of universality and comprehensiveness.

A great High Church controversialist lately confessed that he had come to the conclusion that ' the two schools of thought in the Church of England are permanent and complementary.' They are as necessary to each other in the world of thought as the two sexes in the physical world, and with much the same distinction of natural faculties, those of authority and of sensibility.

Church life would be unhealthy or extinct if either phases were suppressed. Christian spirit would die out if its embodiment were not a partnership, but an absorption, of different characteristics.

## Via Media.

There are, in common parlance, three varieties of Church views—High, Low, and Broad—but the last is a neutral centre between the other two rather than any definite distinction by itself.

Newman dreamt of a *Via Media* between Rome and Canterbury in which Churchmen might meet by agreement to submit their differences to some human authority, though admitted to be fallible. The failure of assumed infallibility disturbed his ideal of Catholicity.

Archbishop Tait's view was that 'there are three phases of thought in the Church. One of earnest persons, thinking more of the deepening of individual spirituality of life; another fostering a reverent love for the corporate work of the Body of Christ; and a third dealing more with the intellectual problems of the day' (*Life*, ii. 297). He thanked God that 'all three schools were now awake,' but added, 'therefore the more need of mutual tolerance and forbearance.' Lord Salisbury took a like view when separating himself from Disraeli's support of Lord John Russell's Ecclesiastical Titles Bill. He described High, Low, and Broad schools in the English Church as its Sacramental, Emotional, and Philosophical divisions; and argued that 'they must always exist, except when any of them may be temporarily crushed by predominant power; as they arise not from any difference in the truth itself, but because the truth must necessarily assume different tints as it is refracted through the medium of different minds.' He added that 'on the frank and loyal tolerance of these schools the existence of the Established Church depends.' Lord Cranbrook, then Mr. Hardy, took the same view, characterising three schools in the Church as those of Ceremony, Enthusiasm, and Free-Speculation.

Dr. Hook considered the English Church as itself the *Via Media* between Rome and ultra-Protestantism which would collide in rancour but for its central position between them. No doubt the English Church is the *Via Media* between Romish and Puritan extremes: and High and Low within it are the two natural components of its genuine entirety. There is no room really for a third party, consisting of a class of men taken separately, who must all belong to one of the other two. Dr. Hook truly says: 'Were all the religionists in the realm to meet and draw up a national form of Christianity, consistent with Scripture and Catholic antiquity, the vast majority would conscientiously prefer our Liturgy and Articles to any other form.' That is to say, that the terms of our Church meet the views of all its members in its composition of differences in detail.

### Christian life is the common aim.

Men of High and Low Church views have equally, if in earnest, the one aim—a Christian life. In both views the Church is the divinely appointed channel of Christian grace; and different conceptions of the means only present the same main object in different aspects. The theological and the ethical aspect affect differently, differently constituted minds.

The Saviour's 'fulfilment of all righteousness,' and His reception of the Holy Spirit's descent upon Him, illustrate severally the objective and subjective aspects, in which all men are drawn to the great Exemplar, 'lifted up' for the imitation of all. Obedience to the Church, and the earnest of the Spirit, are the methods of confidence to walk by the same faith.

The High and the Low Church revivalists alike professed, as their motive, a desire for something more satisfactory to Christian minds in the way of Christian life.

Seek the gift in the means, seek it in the heart, the gift of grace to live aright is the one thing sought by High and Low.

Christians may seek Christ differently, but 'the end of all their conversation is Christ, the same yesterday, to-day, and for ever.'

To the High Church the Low seems a negligent way; and the Low Church accuse the High of 'setting up an unspiritual standard of Church worship.' So Newman was accused, even by Arnold; though his preaching on the 'necessity of holiness for future blessedness,' was the occasion of so inapplicable a comment.

Gore gives the common sense between these views in his No. 1, p. 2, *Bampton Lectures*. Christianity is union by faith in Christ, and if churchmanship assumes, in place of this devotion, the acceptance of a system of theological propositions and ecclesiastical duties, the fruit is of inferior quality. On the other hand, too much stress may be laid on personal feelings and on the assurance of salvation. Christians of different tendencies may obscure the true glory of Christian life. But in spite of obscurations, whether by false ecclesiasticism, Protestant subjectivism, or academic intellectualism, a clear standard of human life was set up by Christ, rather in exemplifying moral principles than by enunciating rules—a life of obedient will. This is a summary of his view, and the substance of this chapter.

## Prayers for Unity.

All Christians pray for unity, conscious of its being the very essence of Christianity. But each naturally prays for it as unity with his own view, and of strict conformity with his own idea, not only in general aim, but in speciality of detail.

It is usual, at a Church Congress, for High and Low churchmen to congregate separately in prayer for union— the High desiring the Low may become High, and the Low desiring the High 'to cease as Ephraim from vexing Judah.' (Bishop Ryle, p. 16.)

No doubt, everybody should wish all others to unite with themselves in everything they consider essentially right. Dissenters of all kinds should wish, if they believe their schism justifiable, that all should unite in their kind of separation. Quakers should desire all the nation, from the Queen downwards, to be Quakers. Methodists must all pray for general nonconformity, which is the only point on which they agree among themselves. But there can be no such mystification between membership of the original Church, and of subsequent sections from it, such as the Apostles expressly protested against, whether special followings of Apollos, Cephas, or of any other man, in whose names none were baptized. Parties within the Church, High and Low, need only pray for unity in the sense of eliminating differences that are vital to Church doctrine between them.

Archbishop Tait, throughout an Episcopate of constant ecclesiastical litigation, so far united parties in the Church as to bring their joint abuse upon himself. This entitles him to credit as a fair exponent of the basis from which contrary extremes depart. He realised, what he always argued for, the essential comprehensiveness of a National Church—a phrase disliked by both extremes, but which nations who have lost it would be happy to recover.

We find ourselves collecting in St. Paul's Cathedral, whenever the whole nation wants to thank, or to propitiate, the Supreme Ruler of our common destinies. If those who have actually separated themselves from the Church find their highest interests at times perforce unite their worship, surely the idiosyncracies within the Church may cease from egotism which exaggerates un-vital differences; and seek for unity, not each with himself but, in catholicity as comprehensive as the Church itself potentially is.

Man has but two devotions—to God or self—and the natural fall is from the higher to the lower level.

## High and Low Church Views may have nothing to do with Religion.

High and Low Churchmen may be equally religious, or they may be equally destitute of religion, as they probably are when self-complacency breeds mutual contempt.

Ordinances, to which the High Church specially look for definite gifts of grace, are recognised also by the Low Church as channels for the inflowing of the Spirit. But as the Spirit may be lost from High Church observances in lifeless formalism, so may Low Church invocations evaporate in empty sound.

Idolatry of the means alone will kindle only the idol spirit. Such worship will be heard according to the idols in the heart (Ezekiel xiv. 4). On the other hand, the aspiration for spirituality may be nothing but the breath itself—*Vox et præterea nihil.*

The higher sense of Church order and ministry may indeed inspire the noblest and most glorious worship, and the simplest oratory may convey to God utterances of the deepest piety. Religion is not necessarily engaged in either process, though its interests may be much concerned in such difference of offerings as may either reduce divine service to be perfunctory, or dissipate it in mere incantation.[1]

But whether sacraments are thought to confer, in the act, mysterious gifts of grace, or merely taken as privileges of Church membership—whether, means of grace are valued as Church appointments, or 'remembered' as the Creator's provision for maintaining the true Spirit in our probationary life—or whether services appeal gorgeously to the senses, or be plain prayer and praise—religion may, or may not, accompany these different ideas, which have nothing certainly religious in themselves. Life may flourish in either view, or death may brood over both. There is no difference between High and Low Church views which can in itself be a test *stantis aut cadentis fidei*, nor can religion be predicated, or prejudged, of either appreciation of its provisions.

## The Mass of Christians in the World are outside any Visible Church.

This discussion suggests that differences between High and Low Church views chiefly come from a difference of

[1] It seems strange to us, now that strife has mitigated, to recall Dr. Arnold's accusation of the reviving High Church, 'That it did not enforce any great point of moral or spiritual perfection which other Christians had neglected, nor in any special manner preach Christ; so offering a striking contrast to the Low Church religious movement' (*Sermons on Christ's Life*, Introd. xxv, 3rd edition). So long did it take even a liberal mind to see the possibility of the same spirit animating or defaulting, in both revivals, as men might be more or less recipient of it.

mental constitution, which alike affects all matters of human interest, and that they need not involve dispute of vital doctrine, nor break community in worship, or cordiality in Christian life.

But this Christian sympathy is not limited to the visible Church, but shared by many unbrought within its doors.

Good men and true, both High and Low, within the Church, have a large brotherhood, alike in sentiment both High and Low, outside.

To repeat Dr. Pusey's words: 'As many members of the Body are not members of the Soul of the Church, who, amid outward profession of the faith, do in heart and deed deny Him Whom in words they worship; so there are many who, though not of the visible Body, are members of the Soul of the Church, in faith, love, and obedience, cleaving to Him.'

These outside members of Christ's Church are either, for some reason, innocently separated from the visible Church, or living where none such exists. There are probably more such unattached Christians in the world than are admitted into the Church by baptism. Certainly there must be many more than all those who are true to their profession.

All true Christians, attached and unattached, constitute together what is called, in the opening definitions, the invisible Church of Christ on earth. Church principles exclude no person of real piety from that communion. There are more fish in the sea than in all nets.

Many are daily gathering in from outside, as the Gentiles first came in spontaneously to the opening doors, and the Church's spirit is widely comprehensive. The Spirit of Christ is nowise confined to the visible Church which He founded for all. The spirit of recent litigation has been a narrow spirit of exclusion, now relenting. The Christian religion is an engagement of men's willing hearts, and exclusiveness is a counter-spirit. Many whom Rome has excommunicated, and Geneva consigned to reprobation, will meet in the end among the redeemed from every nation, when the light of Christ's glorious coming will obliterate traces of mistaken separation, and of supposed wanderings from the appointed way.

## But Voluntary Outsiders are not without Guilt.

Mr. Palmer says (*Church*, vol. i. p. 83, 3rd edit.): 'With reference to those who are not members of the Church, there is a great difference between those who actually apostatize from the evident truth, and those who have been born and educated out of the pale of the Church's teaching, and have indeed imbibed from their parents or instructors doctrines contrary to the truth.'

The Wesleyans best illustrate unjustifiable separation from the Church, and violation of Christian unity without excuse. Their leaders are now boasting, in an unchristian spirit of jealous rivalry, that the New World has so increased their number as to exceed that of the Church. But even if this were true, such a prevalence of special denomination would not alter the general claims of Christian union. A tail becoming the larger part of a body would affect symmetry and damage action, but it would not become the body, nor acquire to itself the character of the body.

But it has been already observed (p. 21) the *soi-disant* Wesleyans are, of all men, the most anti-Wesleyan. If Wesley's spirit is now cognisant of what passes here it must execrate the abuse of his name, and lament the realisation of his greatest dread lest his stirring Church revival might lead to Church disunion.

Wesleyans try to escape from this painful consciousness by a distinction between 'union' and 'uniformity,' which they say Christ did not make an essential character of His disciples. They have, however, deprived themselves of this vain plea by adopting the Church liturgy throughout, so that nothing remains to characterise their separation but simple jealousy. For such intolerance to preach toleration reaches the acme of self-deceit. It is also the inversion of all Christian principle. 'No theory,' says Curteis (*Dissent*, p. 22), 'can fit such facts except that Our Lord knew not His own meaning: and, after planting in the world an institution in which His spirit of love might breathe as vital air, He is now well pleased to see envy and dissension part His Church asunder.'

Is Christ only so 'divided'; is He not rather 'crucified afresh and put to open shame' (Hebrews vi. 6) by professed disciples affecting special devotion in the very act of rending His Body?

The differences of High and Low within the Church seem insignificant indeed compared with such treachery to the first principles of its allegiance. But High and Low Churchmen are not guiltless of the same schismatic spirit who exaggerate the differences of views between them as disputes of principle. The Primate mildly condemns them as 'devoid of all sense of proportion in their estimate of what are matters of importance.'

## Church Parties conflict in the presence of a Common Foe.

Dr. Pusey asked this question in a remarkable letter to the *Record* (February 1, 1864), 'Why cannot the High and Low Church professions of faith combine against the spirit of unbelief?'

Schisms of communion, and even schisms of faith, are not the worst danger to which the Church is exposed. They are of unchristian spirit, but the spirit of infidelity is Antichrist itself. In the words of the Great Judge Himself, 'He that believeth not in the name of the only-begotten Son of God is condemned' (John iii. 18). This fatal faithlessness He predicted as the last stage of the world's corruption before His coming again (Luke xviii. 8).

The early Church had to contend with heathen opposition and persecution. Afterwards danger came from internal controversy, and political corruption. It was in the Church's slumber of last century that the utterly antagonistic spirit of infidelity stalked forth. The pride of advancing science resented the claims of faith. Human reason ran riot in the province of faith, and speculation wandered into regions out of ken.

'The world by wisdom knows not God' (1 Cor. i. 21).

In spite of much recovery from this invasion by rationalism on faith, and of revived recognition of faith's proper claims, there is, at this very moment, sad proof of the damage which has been effected by it, in the extravagant eulogies of M. Renan. They so outrun the maxim of *de mortuis nil nisi bonum* as not even to qualify their praise of his philosophy by any sorrow for his extravagant ridicule of the Christian Creed, though admitted to be a fanciful romancing with no rational substitution for what he sought by scoffing to destroy.

It is marvellous how little permanent effect all the sceptical theories have had on the general faith of mankind. Dr. Dale, in his last valuable little volume (*The Living Christ*) gives the true reason, that faith finds its access through the heart more than head, and one consciously answered prayer convinces more than all argument. The conscience of man responds to his Creator's voice speaking to his experience. 'If any man *will* he shall *know*. Luther asserted that 'an old woman with her Bible in her chimney corner might know more than all theologians.'

Still the spirit of unbelief, whether in form of scepticism, or indifference, is the deadliest enemy to the spirit of religion; and all true liegemen of the Cross, however varied or irregular their ranks, are deeply interested, and bound, to merge their differences in rallying round their common standard for combined resistance to their common foe. While High and Low Church are disputing about the process of new birth, or exact meaning of Real Presence, or the prescriptive wardrobe of priests, or legitimate drama of worship; the world, in Renan's phrase, is 'escaping from the meshes of all belief.' Young ladies are engaged infusing their half conceptions of sceptical theories in attractive little novels: the rattle of a talking age is chattering the fancies of unthinking brains, and the flattery of shallow education, and rejected reverence, all swell the tide of this world's last development against the next world's unflinching claims.

### The Church, as the world widens, needs stronger bonds of union.

If the scattered early Churches preserved unity in the Apostles' doctrine and fellowship only by divine guardianship, how much more must Christ's 'presence to the end' be needed in these days of cosmopolitan development!

In the first planting of the Church, on manageable territory, on the confines of old and coming population, and under cover of universal empire, its growth was both compact, and fed all round. But its cohesion was severely tried in the division of empire; and its community of interest, and supply of sustenance, were threatened by the increasing divergence of nationalities. Differences of language, modes of thought, and habits, endangered the continuance of connection, and strained the symmetry of ecclesiastical system. Only Higher Power could overrule such obstacles to union. The Eastern, Roman, and Frankish characters could not otherwise have blended and coalesced in the Gentile Church. The world's government passed from monarchy to feudalism, and the spirit of coming democracy breathed throughout the world. Papacy lost all semblance of supremacy, and œcumenical councils were succeeded by synods. It was a question whether the synods of separate churches could hold their own, or hold all together. The Church which went out from England to the New World assumed the local spirit of self-government by conventions of delegates, though a cordial intercourse has remained between the Mother and Daughter Church. The synodical action of our colonial Churches is in process of local formation, but in communion with us.

The test of orthodox doctrine has ever been '*quod semper et ubique*.' Now that nineteen centuries constitute the '*semper*,' and a hemisphere is added to the '*ubique*,' how much greater must be the strain upon cohesion, and trial of identity, and how constant the danger of divergence from the standard of faith!

The American Episcopal Church government has revised, without altering, the Prayer-Book of the Mother Church. Pity the name of Protestant is retained by the progeny, which is born into the freedom once for ever gained by its ancestry. Frederick the Great, in some campaign, making a convent his headquarters, found them still praying, after two centuries, for the soul of their founder. 'What,' said he, 'not yet out of purgatory? I confiscate your fruitless charity.' Eternal 'protest' might similarly discredit the success of 'reformation.'

The disestablished Irish Church has also revised the English Liturgy, with only two verbal emendations.

Succeeding Churches must far outnumber the Mother Church. So Alexander's conquests far exceeded the home of his achievements, avert the omen of his scattered empire, over which heaven's guardianship did not preside! If the Church ' but to itself be true,' its Lord has promised that the gates of hell shall not prevail against it. Separate communions, calling themselves Churches, severed ramifications from the original stem, can hardly expect the vital sap to flow in limbs so parted from the stock. They spread, indeed, from out each other, as the fingers of ungenuine roots, which multiply in loss of character. The true Church keeps in fruitfulness the branches 'which abide in it.'

> '*A broken lineage, and a doubtful race,*
> *Can't count on pledges of perennial grace.*'

## But Catholicity forbids Identity both in corporate and individual Communion.

An institution meant to embrace the whole of this wide and varied world to its full development must admit, in all non-essential details, freedom of idiosyncrasies, both national and individual. There can be no identity of type throughout such confederation.

The Warden of Keble College writes, in his article on the Church, in *Lux Mundi*: 'The very fixity of its great central doctrines allows remarkable freedom to individual opinion. As time goes on it is right that the old truths should be elaborated, polished, and adapted. It is wrong that they should be changed, maimed, or mutilated. The claims of the society may be urged too far, to the detriment of the individual. The central organisation may crush out national life, and give no scope for individual development' (pp. 388-9, 396). This view contemplates the Church as not only stretching itself over new diversities of nationality, and among varieties of individuals and circumstances, but as meeting new demands of developing intelligence, and increasing experiences of mankind.

None can suppose that the Creator did not anticipate the full requirements of His spiritual provision for the world's whole history in every phase of its gradual probation. The most senseless cavil of scepticism is that the inspired writings correspond with contemporary limitation of scientific knowledge, which is ordained to be progressive, and which, in its utmost measure, is infinitesimally small after all. This measure Divine Providence has comprehended, but not disturbed, in its revelations from time to time to man. The brotherhood of Churches, as well as the communion of individual membership, merges specialities of circumstance and character in one comprehensive scheme of the Church's commonwealth for all time.

With the dangers of development there accompany advantages of widening opportunities of Christian intercourse, strengthening the whole body, and kindling larger sympathies both in corporate and individual relations.

## True Christian Fellowship.

Christ used two seemingly opposite proverbs on two different occasions. When the Pharisees blasphemed His casting out devils by His Holy Spirit's power, He said, ' He that is not with Me is against Me' (Matt. xii. 30), that is, the rejection of My Spirit is the rejection of communion with Myself. When some who were not followers of Him cast out devils in His name, He said, ' He that is not against Me is with Me' (Mark ix. 39), that is, when My Spirit is not rejected, but invoked, the will, that is the man, is in communion with Me.

Surely Christians may apply their Master's maxims; and though they must consider those who are not with them on points of vital faith, and in the Christian spirit of unity, to be not of their following, yet those who are not following with them, if invoking the same Spirit in the name of Christ, they may consider to be in heart and will with them. Much more may men of only different ways in the same following recognise a full communion, and render without reserve joint homage to the Lord of all.

The Churches of the Old World, and those of the New, different as are their atmospheres both of contemplation and of action, may breathe together the same spirit of catholic Church-fellowship. Among Churchmen individually different modes of mental vision will range from the highest to the lowest appreciation of the Church, yet fail not of the one comprehensive idea; unless evil thoughts of one another, and self-complacency, disprove the dwelling in them of the Church's Spirit altogether.

Christianity is essentially a matter of willing minds, in common devotion to Christ, however differing in their honest conceptions of that devotion.

Some say Christianity is dying out in the world, but it may be hoped, especially from recent appearances, that what is dying out is the taking for Christianity what it is not—namely, speciality of views concerning Christ's Church. High and Low are coming to recognise their fellowship. English Bishops, High and Low, have made great efforts lately, whatever may be thought of them, yet intended, for complete re-union from departures in both directions. But religious differences are not reconcilable by treaty. Such recoveries of peace and unity come silently, and almost imperceptibly. Controversy has done good work in discovering how little has been vital in contention. The chief features of our Church have always retained their pristine type. Churchmen, High and Low, if only in earnest, evince in their lives the universality of the system into which they are incorporated, and to which they all belong.

www.ingramcontent.com/pod-product-compliance
Lightning Source LLC
Chambersburg PA
CBHW020231090426
42735CB00010B/1639